THE SUCCESSFUL EXHIBITOR'S HANDBOOK

THE SUCCESSFUL EXHIBITOR'S HANDBOOK

Profitable marketing techniques at trade or consumer shows

Barry Siskind

Cartoons by Andrew Benyei

Self-Counsel Press
(*a division of*)
International Self-Counsel Press Ltd.
Canada U.S.A.

Printed in Canada

First Self-Counsel edition: September, 1990

Canadian Cataloguing in Publication Data
  Siskind, Barry, 1946-
  The successful exhibitor's handbook

  (Self-counsel business series)
  ISBN 0-88908-885-3

  1. Exhibitions.   2. Selling.   I. Title.   II. Series.
  T396.S57   1990   659.1'52   C90-091334-7

Self-Counsel Press
(*a division of*)
International Self-Counsel Press Ltd.
Head and Editorial Office
1481 Charlotte Road
North Vancouver, British Columbia V7J 1H1

U.S. Address
1704 N. State Street
Bellingham, Washington 98225

CONTENTS

LIST OF WORKSHEETS

LIST OF FIGURES

PREFACE

Welcome to the exciting world of trade and consumer shows.

Selling effectively in international and domestic markets, through the medium of trade and consumer shows, requires the use of skills and techniques that have been developed and improved over many centuries. In fact, many of the basic selling skills used in the colorful eastern markets of antiquity are still widely used today.

Successful selling is an exercise in effective communications between two or more human beings. While the product or service being sold is important, the first priority in any sales effort is to establish a communications link between the buyer and seller. Whether it is the ancient trader in the marketplace calling, "Have I got a deal for you!" or the sophisticated sales representative of today questioning a new prospect on his or her immediate needs, the purpose of the verbal exchange is to establish communication — to create a desire for more information that will eventually lead to a sale.

The Successful Exhibitor's Handbook has been written and designed as a reference book for managers and staff who participate in trade and consumer shows, both at home and abroad.

According to *Trade Show Weekly*, there are more than 10,000 annual shows in North America. Over 100,000 companies participate in these shows and spend in excess of $12 billion exhibiting their wares.

This is indeed big business, yet many companies take a seat-of-the-pants approach to their show participation, especially where support staff are concerned. The principles outlined in this book apply to every staff member who participates in a show. Each must understand the importance of his or her individual contribution.

The contents of this book should be required reading for every person in your company who has any part in your show activities.

To help both neophyte and experienced show participant get the most out of this book, it has been organized into three sections:

PART I — BEFORE THE SHOW: An essential ingredient of a successful show is careful planning and preparation well before show deadlines.

PART II — AT THE SHOW: The all-important skills of selling and working the booth must be properly understood.

PART III — AFTER THE SHOW: All of the time and money spent on the show is wasted if you don't have a properly planned and executed follow-up procedure and an in-depth analysis of the show results.

Use the forms illustrated in the book as part of your own planning and execution procedures. Following the step-by-step guides should result in more profitable and enjoyable shows for all involved. Even though you may not shout the same slogans as the eastern trader did, you will be able to give a professional equivalent of the old "come-on," with high expectations and a smile!

PART I
BEFORE THE SHOW

1
WHY EXHIBIT?

a. GENERAL

A successful show, like any well-executed marketing exercise, starts with a carefully thought out plan of action. Such a plan gives direction to the whole effort, sets goals, and gives you yardsticks to measure your results against.

So, where do you start?

A natural beginning is to ask yourself the question: "Why should I exhibit? What's in it for me, my company, and those salespeople I'm going to take off the road for several days?"

These are excellent questions that should be answered before you spend any time planning to participate in a show. Once you've got your answers, you'll find an added bonus — they give you the goals you need to feed into your overall plan! So don't pass off this initial exercise as a waste of time and effort. If you want to have a successful show, and be able to prove it to those who count, having a clear idea of why you are exhibiting in a particular show is vital to your success.

b. COMMON EXHIBITORS' GOALS

Here are some of the common goals that exhibitors set for themselves when they participate in trade and consumer shows.

(a) Make sales:

Direct

Bookings

3

Follow-up

(b) Introduce new products:

    Show samples

    Free publicity

    Press conference

(c) Meet dealers and representatives:

    Market support

    Product support

    Sales support

(d) Meet customers:

    Prospect lists

    Mailing lists

    Sales leads

(e) Create an image:

    Quality

    Reliability

    Service

    Competitive

    Innovative

(f) Demonstrate a specialized product

(g) Be compared to your competition:

    From customers

    From prospects

    From displays

Since not all of these reasons apply to every exhibitor, let's take a look at each one listed, in detail. You can check off those that apply to your particular case.

1. Make sales

This is probably the most common reason given for entering a show. It does, however, mean different things to different people. If you're a wholesaler exhibiting at a trade show for your industry, making sales could mean booking orders from dealers and jobbers; it could also mean selling products straight from your booth (if show regulations allow).

For some exhibitors, particularly those selling high-ticket items, sales off the floor may not be a reasonable expectation. In this case, their sales goal is to collect qualified leads which will be followed up after the show.

At consumer shows, many exhibitors go with the intent of selling products from their booths. Some products lend themselves to this type of approach, others require follow-up calls to take measurements, choose colors etc.

2. Introduce new products

If you have a new product to bring to market, there's no better place than a trade or consumer show. According to research report #21 prepared by the Trade Show Bureau in 1984, 56% of visitors come to see new products and services.

Show managers often look for new products to feature in their show promotion material, while magazine editors are always looking for new product information to report to their readers.

3. Meet dealers and representatives

You'll find plenty of opportunities to meet and assess the capabilities of potential new dealers or representatives, especially if they are exhibiting at the show. It's also an opportunity for you to show your products and services at their best — in your well-planned booth.

4. Meet customers

The cost of planning, building, and staffing a show booth may seem high, but in terms of the cost per contact made at the show, it's hard to beat.

Your staff has the opportunity to meet existing customers and prospects. According to Trade Show Bureau report #21, 92% of show visitors claimed that they had not been called on by salespeople in the last 12 months.

5. Create an image

While the word "image" means different things to different people, the quality of your display, the behavior and attitude of your booth staff, and the aspects of your product or service that you choose to emphasize all contribute to your image.

6. Demonstrate a specialized product

Shows give you the opportunity to demonstrate to a large number of receptive people in a short period of time. Visitors come to shows to see, feel, touch, taste, and smell your products and services.

7. Be compared to your competition

Intelligent buyers will always compare competitive products. If your competitors are exhibiting, you can also view their products first-hand.

8. Other

You can probably add a few more goals to your own list. When you have completed your list, analyze it carefully. You'll be forced to the conclusion that achieving your goals requires careful planning, training of staff, and post-show review.

c. PLAN YOUR SHOW GOALS

Use Worksheet #1 to set your goals and rank them in order of importance.

WORKSHEET #1
PLANNING YOUR NEXT SHOW

My five goals are: **Rank in order of importance:**

1. _____   _____

   _____

   _____

   _____

2. _____   _____

   _____

   _____

   _____

3. _____   _____

   _____

   _____

   _____

4. _____   _____

   _____

   _____

   _____

5. _____   _____

   _____

   _____

   _____

2

SETTING GOALS

Participating in a show is a marketing decision in the same way that a decision to run an advertising program or a direct mail campaign can be an integral part of your marketing program.

When you went through the exercise in Worksheet #1 of setting out your reasons for exhibiting, your overall marketing plan should have guided you in deciding what you wanted to get out of this year's shows. You now have a good idea of what your goals should be — but how specific can you be at this time? Can you measure them? Are they realistic?

Goals that cannot be measured are not really goals at all, they are vague hopes. Goals that cannot be realized only lead to frustrated staff and lost opportunities. The selection of realistic and measurable goals calls for thorough research and unbiased analysis of your market and the demographics of the shows you plan to participate in.

In this chapter we'll be looking at four stages of goal setting as follows:

(a) Measuring your goals

(b) Setting realistic goals

(c) Ranking your goals

(d) Establishing individual goals

a. MEASURING YOUR GOALS

The reason for measuring goals is to provide a guide for your future show activities. For this reason, your goals should be short term even if your product has a long-term sales cycle.

As an example, a heavy equipment manufacturer may have an 18-month sales cycle but can't wait 1½ years to decide whether the show was worthwhile. In this case, the goal might be measured by the number of qualified leads received at the show.

When you are introducing a new product or demonstrating a specialized product, your immediate goal may not be sales. In this case, your goal could be the number of demonstrations given, or acceptance by a major purchaser or government laboratory for testing.

If you are exhibiting for the first time, your primary goals may be one of the following:

(a) To create awareness of your products and your company

(b) To get a feel for the local market

(c) To find a reliable local agent or distributor

Goals should be quantifiable to be of value. If your goal is sales, measuring is easy — you count the number of orders or sales leads. In other cases, measuring goals can seem very difficult. For example, a participant in one of my trade show seminars sold his products through a network of dealers. His goal was to create an image for his company. When asked how he would know when an image had been created, he replied, "When people see my product and understand how it can help them."

"So, if you can show your product to people who have never seen it before, and they understand how it can help them, will you have satisfied your image need?" I asked.

"Sure," he replied, "I want as many people as possible to know about my product."

"How many?" I asked.

"All 12,000," he replied.

A measurable goal, but far from realistic for several reasons, which is discussed in the following section.

b. SETTING REALISTIC GOALS

Setting realistic goals is just as important to your success as selecting the right goals. If your targets are too low or too easy to attain, you won't feel challenged to perform and you'll probably miss a number of opportunities. On the other hand, if your targets are too high or too demanding, you'll have a disgruntled sales force and a bad feeling about the show.

How do you set realistic goals?

Let's continue the story of our manufacturer, who was trying to create an image for his company.

Reference to the demographics for the show, provided by the show manager, showed that approximately 12,000 visitors attended the show last year. Of these, about 8% were plant engineers — the industry group the manufacturer wished to reach. A discussion with the show manager and several exhibitors led us to the conclusion that this manufacturer could expect 30% to 35% of the visiting plant engineers to pass through his booth. A few quick taps on our calculators and we came up with a figure of approximately 300 leads. After further discussion, he decided that perhaps half of those would be unfamiliar with his product line.

So now, our manufacturer has his goal: to demonstrate his product to 150 new qualified prospects. By setting this goal, he has taken a giant step toward having a very successful trade show.

Even though the manufacturer is happy with the figures quoted above, there's still one very important question that hasn't been asked yet — are the booth staff capable of handling 150 demonstrations during show hours?

Assuming that each salesperson is able to make two presentations during each hour of duty, a twenty-five hour show would require three salespeople on duty at all times to meet the goal.

Whether your target is the number of sales leads, visitors contacted, or sales volume generated, the figures that you come up with should be carefully researched. They should relate directly to the number of visitors that you can realistically expect to stop at your booth, and the booth should be staffed properly to meet your goal.

If you don't have previous experience with a particular show to enable you to come up with reliable estimates, then talk to show management, other exhibitors, competitors, suppliers, and customers.

c. RANKING YOUR GOALS

By now, you probably have between five and ten items on your list of goals. One or two should stand out as being the prime reason for exhibiting. For example, if your purpose for exhibiting is to attract representation then you must ask whether the show will help you find a good agent. Most of your efforts should go toward reaching this goal. If, for any reason, a show does not offer the chance of achieving your primary goals, you should not use that particular show.

The balance of your list of goals should be ranked in order of importance. This calls for impartial judgment and an honest appraisal of the significance of each goal. Some you may have to be prepared to sacrifice in favor of those higher up your list.

d. INDIVIDUAL GOALS

Once you have a clear set of goals that meet the criteria of measurability and realism, the next step is to translate them into personal goals for each member of your show staff. Your corporate goals give overall direction to your show efforts while personal goals act as motivators for each member of the booth team.

Personal goals can be broken down in several ways depending on the specific overall goal that you are trying to meet.

From the previous example, our manufacturer's goal was to make 150 demonstrations during the 25 show hours. Individual goals could be set up as follows:

Each show day: number of demonstrations	50.0
Number of shifts	2.0
Demonstrations/shift	25.0
Number staff/shift	3.0
Demonstrations/person/shift	8.3

From this calculation we can assign an individual goal of 8.3 demonstrations per shift to each salesperson — a goal that is both measurable and realistic.

In our example we have assumed equal traffic on each day of the show. In practice this may not be the case and staffing will have to be adjusted to take account of the historic traffic patterns of the particular show.

Once you have selected a show and have reliable demographic information, it is important that you get your staff involved as early as possible. Explain to them why you have chosen the particular show, what your corporate goals are, and how you plan to measure them.

Having set your goals, your next job is to pick the right show, which is discussed in the next chapter.

3

PICKING THE RIGHT SHOW

Whether there is only one show, or several, that cover the market and audience you wish to reach, the procedures advocated in this chapter are equally applicable. After you have read this chapter, you should be able to make an informed decision about the potential value of any particular show that interests you.

During the last decade, the number of shows in North America has more than doubled. Today, there are over 10,000 shows of all kinds that you can visit each year, each with a character of its own.

Smaller, regional shows usually have promotion budgets that match their potential revenues. The big national and international shows require huge, up-front expenditures to promote them to their widely scattered audiences, as well as large staffs to run them.

In between these extremes are all kinds of shows, some well run, others not so well run. Some have adequate budgets, others try to bootstrap themselves into a sound financial condition. Overseas shows have the added danger of unfamiliar territory.

How do you find the right show and check it out before investing your time and money in it? Preferably, you will follow the four stages which will be discussed at some length:

(a) List and check suitable shows

(b) Check demographics and facilities

(c) Check the fit with your goals

13

(d) Decide how much space to book

Let's take a look at each of these stages in turn.

a. LIST AND CHECK SUITABLE SHOWS

The number of shows covered in your particular field will depend on the market you are trying to reach.

Several publishing companies issue annual directories that list trade and consumer shows. Some cover the domestic market only, others cover world markets. In these directories you'll find a lot of very useful information. Shows are usually listed by their industrial classification, location, number of exhibitors, type of show, number of visitors, total space available, and date. These directories should be your primary source of information.

Secondary sources of information are your own trade magazines, trade associations (which often run their own trade shows), your customers, and local chambers of commerce.

Governments are also an important source of information. They maintain staff at home and abroad whose job it is to keep abreast of all commercial activities within their industrial or geographic sectors.

Once you have the list of available shows, you can quickly screen it for dates that conflict with other plans or are too close to allow adequate planning. For the remaining names on your list, a letter, facsimile, or phone call should quickly bring a brochure (and maybe a salesperson!) giving you full details of the show.

If the show has been established for a number of years and is growing, you can be sure the brochure will tell you. It will also give you a list of exhibitors that have participated in previous shows. If you have any doubts, call up some of these exhibitors and ask for their opinions. You can learn a lot from a few simple inquiries that could save you thousands of dollars in wasted efforts.

If the show company is new or unknown to you, then a more thorough investigation is warranted. It is not unknown for shows to be canceled a few weeks before showtime for lack of bookings or financial difficulties.

Do a credit check on the company. Ask the show manager for a list of exhibitors who have booked to date. If he or she balks, be suspicious. Phone some of the exhibitors on the show list — be sure their attendance is confirmed.

This may seem like a lot of work, but it is worth the effort when you consider the damage a canceled show might do to your marketing program. By then you could have wasted tens of thousands of dollars on preparation and promotion.

With your short list in hand and the show brochures set out around you, you can now proceed to the detail work of studying the demographics of each show.

b. CHECK DEMOGRAPHICS AND FACILITIES

There are two concerns here: first, the demographic profiles of both the visitors and the exhibitors, and second, the type of show and facilities provided by show management. Both sets of concerns are important. Here is a list of questions that you should seek answers to.

1. What type of show is it?

This may seem obvious, but there are some shows where the dividing line between a trade show and a consumer show gets blurred. If you are only interested in selling to the trade, then you may not want a show where the public is admitted at certain hours or on certain days. On the other hand, if you are exhibiting a consumer item at a trade show, you may welcome public attendance at certain times as a public relations gesture.

Choosing the right show

2. Is it regional, national, or international?

Regional shows cater to local markets and are promoted only to that market. National shows are promoted to draw attendance from across the nation. International shows are major events that are designed to attract a large contingent of foreign exhibitors and delegates. They are often coupled with high-profile workshops and seminars and are widely promoted and supported by the government or major industry associations of the host country.

3. What is the exhibitor profile?

This is more than just a list of exhibitors — it is also a breakdown by industry segment (Standard Industrial Classification (SIC) codes, for example). Examine the list carefully. You want to know whether your competitors use this show to sell their wares or if they find some other show more effective. Are the major players represented?

4. What is the visitor profile?

Most show managers provide some form of visitor demographics — from raw numbers to detailed breakdowns by job function, job title, geographical location, and size of company. Your interest here is not only the total number of visitors to the show, but how many are potential buyers of your product, and, of that number, what percentage can you reasonably expect to pass through your booth.

5. How is the show being promoted?

Poor promotion usually results in poor turnout. Most show managers, if asked, will give you details of their promotion program. This should include direct mail, magazine and newspaper advertising, radio and TV spots, and trade association support. You may want to tie your own promotion into some of these programs, especially the pre-show issues that are often produced by related trade magazines.

6. What type of registration system?

There are two aspects to registration systems. First, you want a system that gets visitors in with as little fuss as possible. Second, you need a system that records information for future use and incorporates some kind of retrieval system for use with sales leads. Many of the larger shows use embossed cards or imprinters to record sales leads. Others use codes on the visitor badges. If you expect a lot of leads at the show, then you should carefully consider the type of registration system in use.

7. Are there any other associated events?

Shows often have special events associated with them, such as receptions, awards banquets, high-profile keynote speakers, galas, media conferences, and seminar programs.

8. Is there a technical program?

In some industries, the technical program is a vital part of the show. In other cases, a show may be added on to a technical conference. In either case, the technical content is often the one reason that is given by visitors for attending. Departmental managers are often reluctant to let several of their staff take a day or afternoon off just to walk a trade show. On the other hand, permission to attend a seminar on a subject that is work-related is readily given.

9. What are the show amenities?

As an exhibitor, you may need special services such as compressed air. Is it readily available? What is the loading capacity of the floor? If you have a heavy exhibit, this could be important. What are your electrical power requirements?

How does the show facility cater to a large influx of visitors? Are the restaurant and washroom facilities adequate? Will the visitor be encouraged to spend as long as possible at the show, or will they leave early in frustration or disgust?

10. What are the show regulations?

What are the regulations concerning the height and construction of exhibits? If you already have an existing booth, will it conform? Many regulations are dictated by local fire departments. Is your booth made of fire retardant materials? Other regulations cover the shape of your booth, the height of the sidewalls, blockage of the booths next to you, etc. It pays to read the show regulations very carefully, especially before you design a new booth or enter an unfamiliar show. Regulations are often very rigid and not always at the discretion of the show manager to change.

11. Are show layout and traffic patterns well designed?

The layout of the show can have a noticeable effect on the traffic patterns. As a newcomer to the show, you may not have much choice of booth location. Book early and state your preference as strongly as you can. If you don't want to be anywhere near your competition, let the show manager know.

Many shows try to group similar products together in well-marked locations. While this may put you near your competition, it does have the advantage of drawing all of the buyers of like products to the same area and increasing your exposure.

12. What shipping and receiving facilities are available?

You want your exhibit to arrive in good condition and in time to allow you to set it up properly. If you have a large piece of machinery, make sure that the loading dock and passageways can accommodate it. Beware the exhibition hall that has only one or two loading docks and gives priority to the official carrier! Be especially aware of facilities that are above the ground floor and require elevators. If the facility is a union shop, problems could arise through the use of non-union labor.

13. Is public transportation and/or parking available?

Nothing upsets visitors more than poor and expensive parking facilities. Easy parking is a must, together with a lot of signs to show the visitors where to go. There should be good public transportation or a show shuttle bus to and from the exhibition hall.

Proximity to hotels and airports is also a consideration.

14. Are there prizes for best booth, etc.?

Many show managers organize prizes for best booth, best product, or best international exhibit. You should enter these if you can, for a win means extra publicity.

15. What media coverage will there be?

Check to see if the show manager plans to send out press releases to the local radio and TV stations and the daily papers. If you have an interesting product, you may be included in the show's promotion.

c. CHECK THE FIT WITH YOUR GOALS

You now know which shows meet your goals. However, before making a final decision, contact previous exhibitors and ask them the questions you asked the show manager. They will generally give you honest, straightforward answers. But don't rely on just one or two — you may get a biased opinion.

If you get a negative response, make sure that the fault was not with the exhibitor. When things go wrong, the show manager often gets blamed unfairly for things that were due to carelessness or lack of planning on the part of the exhibitor.

If you get a preponderance of negative comments, then you should check carefully — ask the show manager what he or she is doing about the complaints. If the response isn't satisfactory, look elsewhere.

An ideal way to make a final check is to visit that show as a guest, rather than as an exhibitor. If the show is an annual show, this may be too long to wait for your current marketing plan and you will have to fall back on the opinions of others who have been to the show. As a second option, you may want to visit other shows run by the same management. This would give you first-hand experience of their management capabilities.

If you are able to visit a show before you exhibit, spend a couple of days there. Be aware of the quality of the audience. Study their badges. Talk to other exhibitors. Study the booths and get a feel for what you will be competing with. Spend your two days observing everything about the show, keeping in mind your list of questions.

d. DECIDE HOW MUCH SPACE TO BOOK

Your final decision, before booking your space, is how much space you need, and this ties in directly with your goals.

The standard booth is usually 10 ft. x 10 ft. (approximately 3 m x 3 m), although this may vary from show to show. Space is priced either by the square foot or meter, or by booth according to location and size. Large islands and corner booths often carry a premium and many of the more desirable locations are booked year after year by the same companies. If you want one of these prime locations, you may have to wait until one becomes available.

The following factors will determine the size of booth you choose.

1. Product

If your product is a 50 ft. (15 m) conveyor, you'll need a booth at least 60 ft. (18 m) long. If you have a lot of small items arranged on display boards, then you'll need sufficient wall space to hang them in a pleasing and eye-catching manner. You also need space for literature, a small table, and some chairs. If you have four sales representatives on duty, then you need room for at least eight people to be in the booth at the same time without crowding.

In an average 10 ft. x 10 ft. (3 m x 3 m) booth, it is recommended that there be no more than two salespeople at a time. This number does not necessarily increase proportionately with the size of booth. Other factors such as the space taken up by your displays must be taken into account. For example, a 20 ft. x 40 ft. (6 m x 12 m) booth (equivalent to 8 standard booths), with a walk-through display, could well be staffed adequately with 8 to 10 people.

2. Traffic

The size of your booth must be directly related to the number of buyers you wish to contact during the show. If, as explained in chapter 2, you have determined from your demographic information that you expect your sales staff to talk to 12 to 15 people an hour and to get 5 leads per hour from them, then it is a matter of simple arithmetic to determine how many people you need on duty at a time.

The numbers also tell you that during the busiest period of the show, your booth has to accommodate 9 salespeople, plus visitors. It is not inconceivable that you could have 15 to 20 people in your booth at any one time. And if you want your share of visitors to walk through your booth and not straight by, then it must not look overcrowded or too busy to bother with.

The traffic you wish to handle is the most practical factor in determining booth size. To handle 15 to 20 people, a minimum of 400 sq. ft. (e.g., 40 ft. x 10 ft. or 20 ft. x 20 ft.) or $36 m^2$ (12 m x $3m^2$ or 6 m x 6 m) would be needed, again depending on the size of your displays. This calculation assumes that 50% of the booth area is taken up by your display and allows approximately 10 sq. ft. ($1 m^2$) per person including staff and visitors.

If, for other reasons, you can't have a booth this size, then you should revise your goals or look for another show that allows you to reach this goal.

3. Image

Creating an image can take several forms. If appearing to be bigger and better than the competition is your goal, then your booth size will be determined by what the competition does.

If you wish to be seen as the supplier of a new line of products, then you must take the space necessary to adequately display the products and their salient features.

When you want to be seen as the supplier of a wide range of products, then you need room to display at least a representative sample of those products backed up by adequate literature and catalogues.

4. Cost

The cost of booth space is a small portion of the overall cost of exhibiting at a show. However, the size of your booth does affect the total cost in terms of staffing, travel, booth design, construction, and planning. Compromises are often necessary and this is where you'll find the ranking of your goals (as discussed in chapter 2) will play a very important role.

5. An existing exhibit

Displays can cost thousands of dollars to design and build and are often amortized over several fiscal years. Make sure your design is flexible enough to handle shows of different sizes.

6. Available space

Shows often sell out and have a waiting list. Even booking early in a popular show is no guarantee of getting the space you want unless you have been a regular exhibitor. Show managers naturally give priority to previous exhibitors and often do not allocate space to new exhibitors until after a pre-set deadline has been reached. After this deadline, applications are usually treated on a first-come-first-served basis.

From what we've discussed, you will see that an early and close working relationship with the show management will provide answers to many of your questions and signal potential problems long before they become reality.

If the demographics are not in line with your goals, or other factors make it unlikely that your primary goals will be met, then you should not enter a show, even if your competition is there. Just make sure that your evaluation is accurate and unbiased and that you haven't missed something the competition has spotted. If you're sure of your facts, and convinced that your primary goals won't be met, then spend your money more effectively on other forms of marketing, or choose another show.

4

CONTROLLING THE COST

Since many of the costs involved in exhibiting are fixed well ahead of time, there is a tendency to bypass budgeting and allocate a lump sum for shows. The result is a seat-of-the-pants operation with very little recorded data to fall back on.

Shows should be treated as a profit center. Your show budget helps you focus your activities, keep your team on track, and gives you the tools needed for your post-show evaluation (see chapter 14). What's more, with so many of the costs fixed, budgeting for a show is much less of a guessing game.

Preparing a budget allows you to work through the show on paper, with input from each team member, before committing any funds. This means your budget must be done early — in fact, as soon as you have set your goals and picked the right show.

Early budgeting has several advantages:

(a) It brings the overall program into sharp focus.

(b) You have tight control.

(c) You have time to adjust and make changes without incurring cost overruns.

(d) Services can be ordered well ahead of time, avoiding those rapidly escalating late charges.

To make the task a little easier, you can divide the budget into bite-size chunks, which are discussed in this chapter.

a. SPACE RENTAL

In addition to the cost of your booth space, this item also includes hotel space for your staff, hospitality suites, and space for press conferences. You should be able to obtain firm prices for these items from show and hotel managements.

Show managers often designate one or more official hotels where blocks of rooms at special rates are made available to exhibitors. You should mention that you are exhibiting at the particular show, otherwise you may be told that the hotel is fully booked. Hotels often supply show managers with reservation forms for easy booking.

It can't be over emphasized that early booking is essential if you want to be where the action is. Late bookers often end up in out-of-the-way hotels, which means extra daily traveling and added costs.

b. DESIGN AND CONSTRUCTION

If you are constructing a brand new booth, you should include the cost of all materials and labor involved in designing, manufacturing, setting up, and equipping your booth. Don't overlook things like shelves, tables, carpets, etc., if these items are to be supplied by you. If you plan to rent some items, they should be budgeted under show services.

The full cost of a new booth is often amortized over several shows and only the pro-rated portion is included in the current budget. Where modifications are made to an existing exhibit, or repairs are required, the full cost is usually charged to the current budget.

You should also include in this section the cost of packing cases that will adequately protect your exhibit on its many journeys. If you are also planning to exhibit abroad, consult an expert on the best type of packing to use for overseas shipment.

c. TRANSPORTATION

You have the choice of using a common carrier or a mover who specializes in exhibit transportation.

A common carrier will pick up your goods and deliver them to the receiving area or specified storage area at the show. However, you have no control over how your goods travel from one point to another. If you are shipping from one large metropolitan area to another, your goods will likely be picked up by a local delivery truck, transferred to a large cross-country vehicle, and delivered at the other end by another local delivery truck.

If you have fragile or sensitive equipment, then the official carrier may be your best choice. In some cases you will get direct door-to-door service with the same truck and crew. In other cases, the carrier may consolidate shipments locally, then ship them directly to the show to arrive at the time designated by the show manager.

Official carriers often arrange to consolidate foreign shipments at designated border points, collect the necessary documentation from the shippers, and clear them through customs.

Whichever method you choose, you should consult with your shipper early (make them part of your team), and get an accurate estimate of shipping costs.

One other cost that is sometimes borne by the exhibitor is drayage — that is the movement of your goods within the exhibition hall. Ask the show manager who pays drayage, and if he says you, include it in your budget.

d. SHOW SERVICES

Show services include electrical, plumbing, janitorial, carpentry and security services, furniture rental, and the provision of signs, utilities, audio/visual equipment, photography, and telephones. The contractors who supply these services are often designated by the owners of the exhibition hall through long-term contracts. Neither you nor the show manager may have any choice in the matter. In other cases, some of the contractors may be designated by the show manager, while others may be left to your own choice.

Some services you pay for directly, others are included in the booth space charge. You must read the exhibitor manual carefully to find out what is supplied. Where contractors are designated, show management usually supplies order forms.

If you have doubts about any services, clear them with the show manager well ahead of time. Leaving service orders to the last minute can cost you a hefty premium, and possible delays in obtaining what you need.

e. PERSONNEL

In order to get a true picture of your show participation you must account for the costs associated with the people involved. These costs are usually divided into two categories: direct and indirect.

Direct costs are those related to the show staff. These should include set-up crew, sales, administrative, and registration. In addition, there are those costs related to the booth staff, such as travel and living allowance.

Indirect costs are those for the support people who spend some time organizing and administering show activities. These include secretaries, clerical, and accounting staff.

f. ADVERTISING AND PROMOTION

The opportunities for advertising and promotion in connection with a show are endless. Trade and business publications often have special pre-show issues. Local radio, TV stations, newspapers, billboards, direct mail, and the show guide offer numerous promotion opportunities.

A discussion of show advertising and promotion can be found in chapter 6.

g. MISCELLANEOUS

This is a catch-all category for those one-time expenses you'll incur. Included are items such as speakers, entertainment, insurance, parking, show training, etc.

Worksheet #2 gives a detailed list of items for which you should budget. Notice that there is a second column for you to enter the actual costs and a third column to note the difference. This will be a valuable reference guide for budgeting future shows.

h. SOME TYPICAL EXHIBITION COSTS

In a 1988 research report (Cost Analysis #2060), the Trade Show Bureau noted that the average expenditure for booth space for 248 exhibits in 55 shows over the period 1985 to 1987 represented 24% of the total direct cost dollars spent on the shows. In addition, 33% more was spent on salaries and travel expenses for exhibit personnel.

This means, on average, for every $100 spent on space rental, you can expect to spend a total of $554 on the show as a whole. Use this figure with caution since it is the average of a wide range of shows of varying complexity and size. The pie chart shown as Figure #1 is reproduced from this report.

In particular, amortized construction costs decreased by 26% in the latest report, while show services and transportation showed a combined increase of 52% over the same period.

Since individual shows vary so widely in size, market, and allocation of costs, it is difficult to give firm figures for budgeting purposes. However, many of the costs are readily available from show management and others who have participated in the same or similar shows in previous years.

If you are new to show business, talk to your show manager, other exhibitors, and everyone on your show team. If you keep good records, you'll soon have a valuable body of information and experience on which to base your future planning.

FIGURE #1
HOW THE SHOW DOLLAR IS SPENT

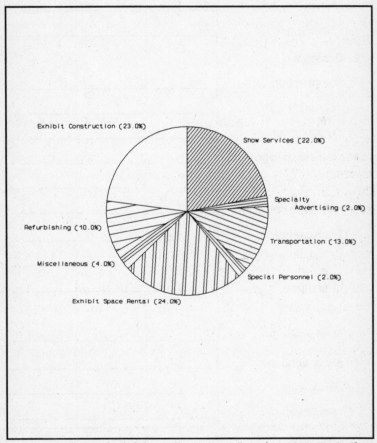

Source: "How the Exhibit Dollar is Spent," August 1988, Trade Show Bureau (Cost Analysis #2060)

WORKSHEET #2
SAMPLE SHOW BUDGET

Item	Budget $	Actual $	Difference (+) or (-)
1. Space rental			
Booth space			
Hospitality suite			
Hotel rooms			
2. Design & construction			
Booth design			
Construction			
Packing design			
Display materials			
Set-up & tear-down			
3. Transportation			
Freight			
Drayage			
Customs & brokerage			
4. Show services			
Electrical			
Plumbing			
Janitorial			
Security			

WORKSHEET #2 — Continued

Item	Budget $	Actual $	Difference (+) or (-)
Utilities			
Telephone			
Equipment rental			
Furniture rental			
Other			
5. Personnel			
Staff salaries			
Temporary staff			
Meals & accommodation			
6. Advertising & promotion			
Print advertising			
Radio & TV			
Direct mail			
Catalogues			
Premiums			
7. Miscellaneous			
_____			
_____			
_____			

5

DESIGNING YOUR DISPLAY TO ACHIEVE YOUR GOALS

The prime purpose of any display is to stand out among competitors and to attract attention quickly. From a quick glance at your booth, visitors must be able to tell who you are, what your product or service is, and how you can help them.

This is easier said than done. With an endless array of design possibilities, general rules to cover all needs are impracticable. To a newcomer, booth design may seem to be a daunting task. However, a well-organized, step-by-step approach will quickly overcome the initial concerns and produce a display that meets your requirements. In this chapter, this step-by-step is discussed.

a. UNDERLYING PRINCIPLES

In many ways, the same principles that apply to the design of effective advertisements can also be applied to the design of an exhibition booth. An advertisement has to grab attention quickly before the page is turned. So let's take a leaf out of the ad creator's book.

Recall one of the lifestyle ads that you regularly see on television or in a magazine. How does it grab your attention?

The story line may be a spectacular sports car being driven through breathtaking scenery; or a family group enjoying an exhilarating cross-country ski. Whatever it is, your attention has now been grabbed and your interest piqued. You stay to listen to the advertiser's message.

The message may be catchy phrases that link the scenes you have just seen to the advertiser's product. While what you see may be seductive or appeal to your fantasies, it creates desire.

The final scene is a call to action. "Buy now!" "Available at your nearest distributor." "Call now, while supplies last." All demand action by the viewer.

Each of the four major sections in these advertisements can be recalled by using the acronym AIDA as follows:

Attract   **Attention**

Build   Interest

Create   **Desire**

Demand   Action

In designing your booth, you should follow these same guidelines. You must attract attention and build sufficient interest for your visitors to look at what you have on display. This helps create a desire and get them further into the booth. At this point you take over and call for action.

b. PLANNING YOUR BOOTH

Your goals are the focal point of all your show planning. Your booth display is no different. Other factors that will impose limits on what you can do and influence your booth are the type of audience, show rules and regulations, and your show budget. Each of these items should be carefully examined before you start designing your booth. So, let's take a closer look.

1. Goals

Your primary show goal should fit into one of four broad categories:

(a) Corporate image building

(b) At-the-show sales

(c) After-show sales or order booking

(d) Lead collecting

Image building calls for excellent graphic displays, videos, and well-prepared salespeople. Sales at the show may require facilities for selling or demonstrating of some kind. Cash and credit facilities with a lot of products on hand will also be required at consumer shows. Order booking and after-show sales still require samples of the product on hand for the customers to handle, with perhaps a demonstration. Lead collecting may call for some form of draw or competition.

As you can see, each goal calls for a very different style of booth.

2. Audience

Your booth must be designed to appeal to your specific targeted market group. Shows segment their audience through their advertising and promotion by age, interest, income, profession, etc.

3. Show regulations

Many shows have regulations that limit the height of booths, especially side panels that may obstruct the view. Other regulations cover the use of music, lights, demonstrations, and anything else that may impede the flow of traffic.

4. Budget

Display costs can have a habit of getting out of hand. Stay within budget, (see chapter 4), and keep close control on expenditures. You may wish to consider the choice of rental, purchase, or lease with an option to purchase as alternatives. Now that you have a clear idea of your requirements, you can start your search for a suitable booth designer.

c. THE BOOTH DESIGNER

It's difficult to choose a booth designer. The large number of shows held each year has created a competitive design industry. You should visit several designers and ask to see examples of their work. Visiting shows is a good way to see designers' work in action. When you see something you like, ask the exhibitors for their recommendations.

Your first meeting with a designer should be exploratory —a chance to find out whether you can work with each other. Set out the ground rules carefully. Ask for a rough layout of the proposed booth with some alternatives. Give as much information as you can from your plan including budgets, audience, and what your primary goal is.

Once you have narrowed your choices down to one or two companies, you can offer to pay them for a more detailed drawing of the proposed booth. This may cost you between $250 and $1,000. One reason for doing this is the flexibility it offers you in buying parts of your booth from other suppliers. If you plan to take this approach, declare it up front so that the booth designer knows what your plans are.

Choosing your booth designer should be done early, certainly no later than three months before the show. This will avoid last minute panics and costly errors and changes.

d. CONSTRUCTION METHODS

An important consideration is the method of building your booth. Are you going to choose a custom-made booth or opt for one of the many systems on the market?

Making this choice is not only a question of cost. The look, size, and flexibility are also important.

Modular systems allow you to enlarge, reduce, or alter the structure of your booth readily. Many excellent displays are made with systems, as a walk around any show will demonstrate. However, while many systems lend themselves quite easily to customizing and allow you to show your individuality, the systems element is still recognizable. If you want something unique, then you'll have to opt for a customized display.

Portability is another consideration, especially if you plan to use the display in several shows. Shipping and storage between shows can be costly. Investigate carefully how the booth will be transported, and what the storage and assembly costs will be. Systems generally are easy to transport, set up, take down, or store. If you order a custom booth, make sure that portability is taken into consideration.

I saved a bundle on this display

e. STYLE

Style is difficult to specify. It's really what suits your industry or market segment and the best way to find out is by visiting shows and observing the style(s) adopted by your competitors. The variations in style are very wide, so don't work in a vacuum.

Once you have established your standards for style, you can then proceed to design a booth that will be attractive to those who attend your show.

One effective method is to create a design that puts your product out of context while still conveying or even emphasizing your message about the product. For instance, you could show a piece of industrial machinery in a quiet country or garden setting, choosing to emphasize the ease of operation and noise reduction features of the product.

If you do choose to put things out of context, be sure your message is clear and doesn't confuse the customer.

f. GRAPHICS

Graphics serve two purposes: first, to stop and grab the attention of people passing your booth; second, to enhance the story you have to tell about your products or services.

The key to good graphics is brevity.

As a means of identification you should use bold and easily recognized names and logos.

To emphasize the main selling points of your product or service, stick to essential facts presented in an easily and quickly readable manner. Make one strong statement, rather than ten weak ones. If you can tell the story better with a picture, do so.

Color is generally more attractive than black and white. Don't ignore the value of three-dimensional models with cut-away views, or mirrors to show what's behind. Use signs to point out new or interesting features of your products.

The choice of media for your graphics is wide and should be made to suit the application and the audience.

Among the media you could consider are silk screens, enlargements of black and white or color photographs, transparencies, cut-out letters, appliques, enlarged reproductions of many different typefaces, and vinyl letters. Each serves a different purpose both aesthetically and in terms of information transfer.

If you don't feel competent in this area, or you feel that your booth manufacturer doesn't have the necessary expertise, then use another company for the graphic design. This is why we suggest retaining the flexibility to choose the best people for each stage of your booth design and manufacture. While there are many companies that can provide full service, there are others whose talents are limited to specific areas.

Here are some other pointers to good graphic design.

1. Corporate logos

Don't overemphasize your corporate logo. Remember that the purpose of this exercise is to convey information quickly to the passer-by. If your company's name is a household word, as many large consumer brand names are, then make it as big as you like. In this case, everyone will know what you are selling.

2. Letter size

If the letters are too small, you will have a problem of readability from a distance. If they are too large, they may overshadow any other messages you are trying to deliver as well as reduce the amount of copy space available.

Figure #2, originally published in *The Exhibit Medium* by David Maxwell, sets out the relationship between letter size and the minimum distance at which it can be seen clearly by a person with normal eyesight and under normal lighting conditions. The distance refers to how far away the reader is from the message. The letter size refers to readable size at those distances. Measure the depth of your booth and the width of the aisle to arrive at the maximum distance you must take into account when calculating letter size.

FIGURE #2
RELATIONSHIP OF LETTER SIZE TO READABILITY

Distance		Letter Size	
Feet	Meters	Inches	mm
10	3.05	5/16	7.9
20	6.1	11/16	17.5
30	9.1	1 1/16	27.0
40	12.2	1 3/8	34.9
50	15.2	1 11/16	42.9
60	18.3	2	50.8
70	21.3	2 1/4	57.15
80	24.4	2 1/2	63.5
90	27.4	2 3/4	69.9
100	30.5	3	76.2

Reproduced with permission from Successful Meetings © 1978, Bill Communications Inc.

The thickness of black lettering should be approximately 1/5 to 1/6 of the height.

g. LIGHTING

When properly and professionally done, lighting can give your booth mood, highlight important areas, and attract visitors. Skimped and improperly placed lighting can make your booth unpleasant to visit and keep visitors away.

Lighting also affects the people working in the booth. Proper lighting can make your booth a pleasant and inviting place to work. If improper it can be hot, unbearable, and a strain on the eyes, leading to headaches and short tempers.

Mood can be created with spots, floods, or colored lights depending on the effect desired. Halogen lights are now very popular because of their reduced power consumption. One 600-watt halogen bulb can adequately light a 10 ft. x 10 ft. (3 m x 3 m) booth.

When placing lights, look for shadows and blind spots and adjust accordingly. You may want to try suspended or indirect lighting to create the desired effect.

By building your booth ahead of time and having a dry run before it is shipped to the show, you can work out any design or lighting problems. All electrical wires and outlets should be hidden for safety and aesthetic reasons.

h. COLOR

The psychological effects of color are well known. With the right choice of colors you can create a mood or theme. Color should not be treated on its own but as an integral part of the overall display mix of graphics, lighting, sound, and video. Each element of the mix can complement or work against the other, so careful consideration of all items is a necessity.

Certain colors may be dictated by the corporate logo but should not be so strong as to overpower everything else. Bright colors such as red and yellow are naturally attractive. So are greens and blues for outdoor themes. Earth tones might be used for food themes, white for winter scenes. Don't use colors such as purple and black that have morbid overtones. Avoid setting signs against backgrounds that make the copy difficult or impossible to read. Use a color wheel, a tool used by interior designers, to select colors that work with one another. Color wheels are available at art supply stores or the booth designer may have one.

i. DEMONSTRATIONS

Demonstrations give you the opportunity to show your customers and prospects your products or services first hand.

Many visitors come to shows for this very reason. The ability to see, feel, and perhaps operate a product is very attractive; so is the opportunity to have it demonstrated by an expert who is available for questioning.

If you plan demonstrations, space must be allocated for groups of people to sit or stand. Many show managers require that demonstrations do not block the aisles. Whatever you demonstrate, it must be visible to all members of the expected audience. Use an experienced demonstrator and create your show with the needs of the audience in mind.

1. Videos

If your product or service doesn't lend itself to a live demonstration, a video can be a good substitute.

To retain interest, videos should be no longer than 90 seconds and should be on a continuous loop. Booth personnel should be familiar with the operation of the monitor and be able to make any necessary adjustments. There's nothing worse than a fuzzy screen.

Videos vary in price depending on length and quality of production. However, a well-made video can be used many times and its cost amortized over several shows. It may also be suitable for use as a field sales tool which will further help justify the cost.

Once again, careful planning of your video is required. Make sure that you focus on your goal. Keep out extraneous material and keep it brief, interesting, and to the point. A professional video production company will help you do this.

2. Sound

The use of music, talking displays, or other forms of sound reinforcement are allowed at some shows and can be used to attract attention. However, many shows have strict rules designed to prevent annoyance to other exhibitors as well as visitors, so check the rules carefully before planning anything of this kind.

j. ACCESSORIES

All the design care and expertise in the world won't make your booth look good if you forget to provide for the storage of stationery, boxes of literature, lead files, etc. Usually, if you put cupboards and drawers in at the design stage, you can find a lot of corners or other spaces that don't take away from your display space. Make sure you train your staff to keep items such as staplers, pens, premiums, tape, coats, and briefcases in the places designed for them. Odd items like these left lying around can quickly make your booth look sloppy and unprofessional.

1. Carpets

Carpets not only make your booth look good, they help to reduce the fatigue from standing on concrete floors all day. If you buy your own, make sure that it is taped down all round with double-sided tape. If you rent, the installer will look after this. Don't use carpets with open loops — women's high heels are apt to get caught. If you can't find an appropriate plush carpet, use a good quality pad under your carpet.

Carpets should be cleaned every day either by your own staff or janitorial services where available. If you own your own carpet, it should be shampooed every two to three shows.

2. Plants and flowers

Plants and flowers help give your booth a warm and inviting look. Positioning is important. Make sure they don't interfere with traffic flow or obscure part of your display. Under the hot lights and hostile environment flowers need constant care to survive. If you choose artificial plants, make sure they are of good quality.

3. Telephones

If you need a telephone, make sure that it doesn't detract from the look of your booth. A growing trend is for exhibitors to use portable cellular phones. However, you should be aware that these instruments do not give good reception in some exhibition halls where interference levels are high.

k. SETTING UP

An important consideration when planning your booth is whether you will be exhibiting in union or non-union halls. If you try to employ a non-union display company to set up your booth in a union hall, you could precipitate a wildcat strike and you could end up paying for extra union labor. Local attitudes vary widely and while many union shops will not object to you using your own staff for setting up, they will object strongly to the use of non-union display companies, so check first.

When you contract out the design and manufacture of your new booth, you should discuss the problems of setting up and taking down with the contractors. If you are planning to have your own staff do this, you must make sure that the design lends itself to easy assembly and disassembly. Where a booth is intended for use in a number of cities, there is a great probability that different people will be setting up in different locations — not all of them with the same mechanical abilities.

The best solution to this problem is to have one staff member who is familiar with the set-up procedures present at all shows. If this is not possible, then foolproof set-up and tear-down instructions should be provided.

l. SHIPPING CONTAINERS

The shipping containers should be designed and manufactured at the same time as your booth. Remember that their primary purpose is to protect your display against damage, so you can't afford to skimp. A secondary consideration is ease of handling.

Among the many varieties of packing cases that you see at a show, there are four broad groups from which to choose:

(a) Custom-designed, self-contained booth (self-pack unit), where the shipping crate is also the booth. When opened up, the crate becomes a freestanding booth or part of a booth.

(b) Custom-designed individual packing crates made specifically for your booth. The crates should be prominently labelled inside showing the location of all components and the proper packing procedure.

(c) Pre-fabricated packing cases in a series of standard sizes. Inserts hold you products and prevent movement inside the case. These cases are often made of molded plastic and store easily.

(d) Systems packing cases. Each system manufacturer offers packing cases that have been custom designed to hold their system. When you buy one of these systems, you have the option (recommended) of buying the packing case(s).

All packing cases should have adequate systems of labeling and numbering for both forward and return shipments.

m. DESIGN SCHEDULE

Once you have selected a contractor to design and manufacture your booth, set up a realistic schedule for its completion. Allow at least three months for it to be built including time for reviews of things such as working drawings, artwork, videos etc. If you want a dry run and a familiarization program for your staff, you should add extra time for this and any last minute changes that may be necessary.

6

PROMOTING YOUR EXHIBIT

As we saw in the previous chapter, promotion plays a large role in the success of any show and requires the active participation of both show management and exhibitors. You can maximize the effectiveness of your own promotional efforts by making them complementary to those of the show manager, as well as other exhibitors.

While the show manager's goal in promoting the show is to get the right audience to attend in large numbers, your goal is to get a select number of that audience who are prospective buyers of your products or services to visit your booth.

In a 1982 study for the Trade Show Bureau, Robert T. Wheeler identified eight factors that influenced visitors to trade shows:

(a) *Obligation* was the most important influence for 25% of respondents. They regarded visiting the booth of an existing supplier as "an obligation of past business activities."

(b) *Habit* was the second most important reason quoted by 23% of respondents. They looked forward to visiting regular exhibitors every year.

(c) *Personal invitation* was third with a 15% response, underlining the value of extending personal invitations immediately before the show.

(d) *Trade journal publicity* came next with 12% of the respondents who reacted to advertisements or editorial copy in a trade journal.

(e) *Other advertising* brought in another 9%. This includes radio, TV, billboards, other magazines, etc.

(f) *Mail invitations* or other promotional literature sent by mail also resulted in a 9% response.

(g) *Recommendations* from associates were listed by 4% of the respondents.

(h) *Not sure* was given by the remaining 3%.

The first two categories in this list account for almost half the visitors to a booth, emphasizing the importance of letting your customers and prospects know where you are and what new products you have to excite them this year.

Although we don't have statistics available for consumer shows, it is reasonable to assume that similar considerations motivate people at these shows. How many times have you said, "Let's go and see what 'so-and-so' has on display this year." Habit and familiarity with suppliers and their products are always good drawing cards — if you dangle the carrot of exciting new things to see. People soon tire of seeing the same things year after year.

Planning your show promotion activities can be divided into three broad categories: pre-show, at the show, at the booth.

Each category should be regarded as a stepping stone to the next category, and none should be neglected. Each activity should be a well-orchestrated event with every facet planned and coordinated to complement your other activities so that the whole comes together as a professional and highly successful presentation of your products or services.

a. PRE-SHOW PROMOTION

Your objective here is to let as many prospects and customers as possible, know that you are participating in the show, where you will be located, and why they should make sure they visit your booth. You should generate some excitement

46

and expectations by describing briefly new products, features, or benefits — and don't disappoint them when they show up.

The various means of promotion are discussed in detail below. Remember to try and dovetail them into the show manager's promotion plans so that they complement one another.

1. Direct mail

For existing customers, direct mail should be designed to reinforce their feeling of obligation to visit your booth.

For prospects you can use mailing houses, publishers, and list brokers. If available, you can pick names from the list of last year's attendees provided by the show manager.

Whichever lists you use, always direct your promotion to a specific person by name. Direct mail that is not addressed to a person more often than not gets "junked." If your list is missing some names, then it's worth the time and effort to phone the company and find out the name of the person to whom you should address show information.

2. Telemarketing

As the results of the survey quoted above showed, as many as 15% of your visitors are influenced by personal invitations. Telemarketing is one of the best means of conveying personal invitations, provided it is done professionally.

Your telemarketing script should be carefully planned and prepared. It should be targeted to the person receiving the call. This may mean preparing several different scripts — one for manufacturers, another for wholesalers, and a third one for retailers. Each script should outline the benefits of your product or service to the person being called, and it should be phrased in such a way that the person's interest is gained very quickly.

The script should also request some form of response from the prospect, such as:

"Good morning Ms. Jones, I understand you're attending the industry show on behalf of your company, is that correct?"....."Great! While you're there I would like to extend an invitation to visit ABC company's display in booth 303. You'll see something there I know you'll find very exciting. It's sold over a million pieces in a related market and our studies show that it has similar potential in your market. Can you tell me which day you plan to attend...?"

When you list the one or two benefits that relate most strongly to your prospect, you should phrase them in a manner that will arouse their curiosity as in the example above. Benefits can include show specials, give-aways, or special product introductions. Use the benefit that will appeal to the person you are calling.

In some markets, you may have to be very specific, so make sure that your telemarketer has all the necessary information readily available.

3. Appointments

Some people prefer to make appointments to see specific exhibitors and thereby avoid the crowds and waiting that inevitably go with a busy show. Appointments can be made by your representatives in the field or by your telemarketer. In the telephone conversation in the previous section, after the prospect had indicated on which day she planned to attend the show, the telemarketer could have continued like this:

"Good. Tuesday, as you know, is a very busy day at the show and we're expecting loads of people. If we can make an appointment for a specific time, I will make sure that one of our representatives will be available to demonstrate this exciting new product and save you having to wait around. What time will be better for you, morning or afternoon?"

4. Magazines and business papers

Most shows have several magazines or special interest publications that cover the fields of interest of attendees. This interest is fostered by advertisements and editorials that are specifically targeted to their field and is supported by detailed demographic data available from the publisher.

Many publishers prepare special pre-show editions of their publications that are often bumper issues. This allows the publisher to give in-depth coverage of the show in the form of detailed listings of the exhibitors and products. These editions are usually distributed shortly before the show and help visitors locate the booths they wish to see and plan their visit beforehand.

Because of the high profile accorded by the editorial coverage of the show, many exhibitors prepare special advertisements for these pre-show issues, often highlighting their exhibit and always inviting the visitor to see them at booth number "###."

If you have something new or special, contact the editors of the magazines and offer them information on the product for inclusion in their pre-show issue.

The editor may ask you to write it up and send it in, or a staff member may be sent to your office to get the story first-hand. Many editors send out letters soliciting information for these special issues. This is an opportunity you should make the most of. Editors welcome well-written, factual copy supported by professional photographs. If it fits the editorial profile of their publication, they'll most likely use it, so study the style of each publication before you prepare anything.

5. Press releases and press kits

These are powerful promotional tools which can get you publicity that would otherwise cost thousands of dollars to buy.

Your press release must be sent to the various editors in time to meet their publication deadlines. Check beforehand to determine the proper dates.

At your show, make sure copies of your press release are placed in the media room. Most shows have a room set aside for the press which is usually staffed by a person whose job is to help the press cover the show.

Releases can vary in size from single-page announcements to elaborate multi-page presentations in attractive folders. Choose whatever you feel the occasion demands (and your budget supports). Here are some basic rules that should be followed in the preparation of these important promotional tools.

(a) If you haven't anything really worthwhile to say, don't say it! Editors are busy people. They get hundreds of press releases each week. They want solid information for their readers and anything in the nature of a "puff" heads straight for the round file. Even worse, anything you submit in future probably won't rate more than a glance. So, review whatever you write dispassionately, or better still, get a colleague who isn't as involved as you in the product to review your release and tell you whether it's worthwhile.

(b) Remember "KISS" (keep it short, stupid). Long rambling releases don't get read. Make your opening sentence a real grabber to get the editor's attention.

(c) Every press release should have a first page (it may be the only page) that contains the following:

(i) Company name, address, contact name, phone and facsimile numbers.

(ii) Title of release, date and city of issue, name of company official making the announcement, name and date of show.

(iii) Brief description of product, its importance, features, comparison with current products, benefits and market at which it is targeted.

(iv) Availability, delivery and price.

(v) Brief description of company, its products and market.

(vi) List your booth numbers at the show.

(d) Establish a working relationship with the editors of the publications that are most important to you. Find out from them how they like to receive material, what their current editorial requirements are, when their deadlines are, and what shape, color, and size of photographs they prefer.

(e) Don't assume that because you're an advertiser you'll get preferential editorial treatment. Many editors resent this kind of pressure. If you have a product that is of interest to the readers (and you should if you're an advertiser), and it is presented in a factual, professional manner, then it will be used whether you are an advertiser or not.

(f) Always address the release to a specific person. If you don't have a name, then take the time to get one. A phone call should suffice, or a look at the masthead of the publication. Some publications have a number of editors and it is important that you get the right one. Otherwise your release may get sidetracked and not reach the right editor until an important deadline has passed.

6. Cooperative advertising

There are many opportunities for cooperative advertising that have the advantages of lower cost to you for a share of more prominent advertisements. They range from a manufacturer sharing space with distributors, to groups such as association members or government trade missions.

7. Other materials

Show managers often provide other materials, sometimes free of charge, that you can use. These include stickers to place on your stationery, pre-registration cards, mailers and invitations to special events. You should take advantage of these offers as part of your pre-show promotion.

b. PROMOTION AT THE SHOW

You'll find several opportunities to reinforce your pre-show promotions while the show is on, both inside and outside the exhibition hall. They should help remind those you have already contacted to visit your booth and attract others who were missed by your pre-show promotions.

1. The show guide

Every visitor gets a show guide, which makes it an excellent vehicle for advertising. The listings of exhibitors and their products are usually free.

Advertising is sold by the publisher of the show guide. This may be the show manager or some other company, such as a publication house, which has contracted to do the job. Some show guides also carry short features on the more interesting new products. Once again, it pays to be in contact with the editor.

2. Press room

Many shows have a press room that is available to you for interviews with journalists. Copies of your press kit should also be available in the press room. Since there will be dozens of other companies' kits laid out alongside yours, an attractive, eye-catching folder will help make yours stand out among the crowd.

3. Seminars

A good program of seminars will help attract many visitors to a show who otherwise may not have come. For exhibitors who sponsor seminars, it helps raise their profile, gives them an opportunity to focus on certain products, techniques, and applications in detail to a large group, and gives them the chance to invite more people to visit their booth after the seminar. If you sponsor a seminar, make sure that you have a good speaker who knows the subject well and can answer questions convincingly.

4. New product displays

Show managers sometimes set up displays of new and interesting products including "Best of Show" awards. They are often placed in areas of the show where show management wants to build traffic. The displays are usually well promoted and can be a valuable source of extra promotion for you. If you take advantage of this offer, be sure to include your company name and booth number in the display.

5. Billboards

These are seen outside the building, in the parking lots, and at approaches to the exhibition halls. In these situations they will be seen by a large number of the visitors to the show.

6. Hospitality suites

Before setting up a hospitality suite, it's wise to check with the show manager. Some shows have rules that prohibit the use of hospitality suites during show hours.

The success of a hospitality suite depends very much on the people who run it. You should try to create a warm, friendly atmosphere where customers and prospects can relax and quietly talk about your products or services. You should have product information and knowledgeable people available to answer questions.

7. Other ideas

Some other forms of promotion include the use of theme characters to hand out invitations or buttons, robots that wander the aisles, advertising in show dailies, handouts in official hotels, bulletin boards to post notices for agents, reps, etc. Before you plan any of these forms of promotion, check with management to see if what you have in mind is allowed. Most shows have strict rules covering these other activities and it's wise to check before you spend any time or money.

c. PROMOTION AT THE BOOTH

Once visitors have found your booth, you must do something to keep them there for a while. While not all of your visitors will qualify for a full presentation, many of them will be potential future customers and you want to make sure they remember you.

1. Premiums

The best way to make a lasting impression is with your personal sales approach that is discussed in chapters 9 through 12. Memories, however, are short, so it is a good idea to give them something tangible such as a pen, letter opener, etc., that will remind them of you in the days and months ahead. Here are some guidelines for using such premiums:

(a) Always print your company name and phone number on the premium. If it doesn't lend itself to an imprint, then it's not a good premium.

(b) The premium should tie in to your product somehow. Car dealers give away key chains because you need a key to start your car. If you can't find something, then put a short sales message on a pen or luggage label.

54

(c) Don't lay them out in dishes or piles for anyone to pick up. That gives the premium little value in the eyes of the visitor. Only give them out to people who show interest in your products. You could say something like:

"Thank you for visiting our booth. As a new customer, we would like you to accept this token of our appreciation."

By restricting the availability of the premium and tying it into a specific interest in your products, you have given the premium value in the eyes of the customer who is more likely to appreciate the gift and remember your company.

2. Demonstrations and samples

Visitors come to shows to see, hear, feel, taste, and smell things. They are looking for a complete sensory experience of products and services. All it takes is a little creativity and imagination to adapt your exhibit to a live demonstration.

Choose your demonstrator carefully. Demonstrators should be knowledgeable, articulate, able to think on their feet, comfortable talking to crowds, and able to project a favorable image of your company.

After the demonstration, if it makes sense, you can give samples to those who stopped to listen. If samples are not practical, hand out a suitable premium.

3. Literature and price lists

Specification sheets, catalogues, brochures, and price lists should be treated in the same manner as premiums. If you give them out to everyone, or lay them out for anybody to pick up, most of them will end up in the garbage.

A much better method is to mark a few copies in bold, bright letters:

BOOTH COPY

Please do not remove

Place these copies strategically throughout your booth. Have a few spares in your brief case for immediate needs. When people show interest you can offer to mail them a copy after the show. If you promise to mail a copy to your qualified visitors, then it gives you a firm lead and reason to follow up.

4. Special events

Some shows stage special events at well-advertised times. These may take the form of a fashion show, a stage show, demonstrations, etc. By participating in these events, you can draw attention to your own booth or products.

One toy manufacturer, I recall, had a line of juggling products. He staged a series of juggling demonstrations that created a lot of interest.

5. Celebrities

High-profile people such as movie stars, athletes, politicians, business leaders, magicians, clowns, and local heroes have drawing power and can bring crowds to your booth. They can sign autographs, speak, entertain, or demonstrate. Whatever they do, make sure that the times of their appearances are well publicized and that the local media is invited. You might also want to arrange a press conference for the radio, TV, and press to interview the celebrity. Make sure that your company name and product is mentioned in all presentations and press conferences.

Among the crowds you attract will be a lot of curiosity seekers. Be on the lookout for those who show some interest in your products and be prepared to approach them as soon as the celebrity is finished. Construct a good opening line, as discussed in chapter 9, and begin the process of qualifying the prospect.

6. Models

Attractive models can have a positive effect on your exhibit if there is some reason for them to be there. I once saw a model sitting on top of a display case. She was there to make the point that the case was strong enough to withstand her weight. She was well dressed and able to answer customers' questions.

In many other cases where scantily clad models are used for the "cheesecake" effect, that's generally all the visitor remembers. Ask what the product demonstrated was, and in most cases he or she won't remember! Models should not detract from the product or service being shown but should complement it.

7. Contests

Before embarking on a contest, you should carefully review your goals for the show in relation to the contest. You should also review current laws at federal and local levels that regulate the staging of contests and make sure that what you propose is strictly legal.

If your goal is to collect new names for your mailing list and you are satisfied that the expected audience meets your broad criteria, then any sort of contest where the visitor is encouraged to place his or her business card or name into a box can produce the desired results.

One problem with this type of contest is the number of unqualified leads that you get. Careful design of your contest will exclude those who would not meet your criteria.

A few years ago a community college decided to run such a contest with the purpose of gathering names of prospective students. The prospects would later be contacted by phone and asked to enroll.

The first time the college offered a television set as first prize. Over 3,000 names were entered. When the entrants were contacted, the most common response was, "I just entered to win the TV."

On their second try, the college offered a $500 scholarship. The number of entrants decreased dramatically, but the number of enrollments showed a marked increase.

Draws and contests can be an effective promotion tool only if they relate to your product or service and the entrants have a greater interest than just winning the prize.

We have covered a wide variety of promotional activities. Not all of them will be applicable to your business. However, it cannot be emphasized too strongly that your success as an exhibitor can be considerably enhanced with a well-planned and coordinated promotional plan that is designed to help achieve the goals you have set for the show.

PART II
AT THE SHOW

7

FINDING THE READY BUYER

Of the thousands of visitors who attend a show, only a small number are *Ready Buyers*. One of the toughest problems facing you is to conserve your energy so that you don't burn out before the end of the show. You must learn how to pick out from the crowds passing your booth those visitors who are potential buyers of your product and not just "lookers."

You are looking for what we call the *Ready Buyer*, that is, the person who is ready to buy now or in the near future. These are the people with whom you must spend your time and energy by first establishing a rapport and then making effective sales presentations.

This chapter looks at the ways of finding your *Ready Buyers* quickly and effectively.

a. TRAFFIC PATTERNS

For the purpose of this example, let's assume that you're expecting 30,000 visitors to your next 3-day show. If the show is open for a total of 25 hours, that works out to an average of 1,200 visitors per hour, or 20 visitors per minute passing your booth.

We know from past experience that the traffic varies considerably from day to day and from hour to hour. Using this experience, you can come up with your own average and maximum and minimum traffic flows as discussed earlier in chapter 2.

Another aspect of the traffic flow problem is the length of time you have available to make contact with each of those 20 visitors as they walk past your booth.

Let's try an experiment. Assume that the section of your booth that you are staffing is 10 feet (3 m) wide. Mark out that distance on the floor of your office and pace the distance slowly, as if you were walking the aisles of a show, and count off the seconds as you go by. You'll probably come up with an average time of between 3 and 4 seconds to cover the 10 feet (3 m). That's not long, is it?

Remember, that's how long it takes someone to walk by your booth. If the visitor shows any interest at all, then you must move quickly to establish communication and determine whether or not you have a *Ready Buyer*. Methods of doing this are described in chapter 10.

b. THE PRESENTATION TRAP

Not everyone who shows an interest in your display is a *Ready Buyer* and therein lies the danger of overextending yourself.

I came across a good example of this recently while attending a boat show. I was there to look, drool, and dream, not to buy. I already have a small boat but I fantasize about owning a larger one with all the latest bells and whistles.

As I was walking the aisles, I saw the boat that dreams are made of. I stopped to look.

"It's a real beauty, isn't it?" said a proud voice at my side.

"You bet it is!" I replied.

The sales representative then began to tell me all about the boat. He described in some detail the latest features that had been included to make the boat as easy to operate as possible. He described the safety features, recent design changes, and was so caught up with his enthusiasm for the product that I had difficulty breaking in to tell him that I was only interested in looking at the boat, not buying.

While listening to this presentation it occurred to me that if this salesperson did this to everyone who stopped to look, he would be worn out long before the five-day show was over. Moreover, he'd be so busy talking to people like me that he'd miss the real buyers as they walked by, and he'd have run out of steam by the time he found one!

Salespeople should also be careful not to appear too hungry or desperate for business. Untimely presentations often give this impression.

The way to avoid this trap is to learn how to recognize the *Ready Buyer*.

A *Ready Buyer* is defined as someone who is ready to buy now, or within the next 60 to 90 days. The length of time may vary, however, with the type of product that you are selling. For example, if you sell airplanes and the sales cycle is two years, then your *Ready Buyer* has a time span of from now until two years hence. On the other hand, if you sell photocopiers with a 30-day sales cycle, then you are looking for those who will buy within the next 30 days.

Knowing the average length of time it takes you to close a sale from your first contact will tell you how to define your *Ready Buyer*.

In order to obtain and analyze information quickly, your communications skills need to be sharply honed. You must be able to ask the right questions in a manner that encourages prospects to give you meaningful answers. The best way to do this is to develop good rapport.

c. DEVELOP RAPPORT

Think about the last time you bought something.

Who did you buy from? ... A salesperson you liked?

Why did you buy? ... Was the salesperson easy to talk to?

As a salesperson at a show, you don't have the time to develop relationships, so you must move quickly to make the atmosphere friendly, relaxed, and conducive to conversation. You have to build a trust — this is called rapport.

Webster's Dictionary defines rapport as "...a relationship marked by harmony." It is often described by saying that someone "is on your wave length," or that you "have good vibes," or other similar sayings. In other words, there is a positive feeling between two people that is conducive to sharing of information.

Building rapport is not easy to do, but there are some well-researched techniques that have been found to work and are used to varying degrees by salespeople, both consciously and unconsciously, every day. Even if you are a skilled salesperson, these techniques are worth reviewing to see where you can hone your skills.

At a show, the following things work against the development of rapport between prospects and exhibitors:

(a) Time — As discussed in the previous example, there just isn't enough time at shows to deal with people the way you would normally.

(b) Fatigue — The show is an unfamiliar environment. Toward the end of a long and grueling day, both you and your prospects are liable to be tired and irritable.

(c) Attitude — You may encounter a prospect who has just left a particularly pushy and annoying salesperson, or is disappointed at not finding something he or she was hoping to see.

Developing productive communications under such circumstances requires sensitivity, perception, and the use of non-verbal as well as verbal skills.

Non-verbal messages are communicated to another person by dress, mannerisms, body language, expressions, and gestures. The old saying that "opposites attract" is a long way from the truth under show conditions. People feel far more comfortable talking to those who appear to have similar values to their own.

Human nature is such that we gravitate toward familiar things rather than those that are unfamiliar. So, trying to see things in the way your prospect sees them helps to create a bond of familiarity and enhances the probability of meaningful and productive conversation.

d. ASSESS YOUR POTENTIAL CUSTOMERS

How do you quickly learn what your prospects' thought processes are? Two California researchers — Richard Bandler, a linguist, and John Grinder, a mathematician — studied the relationships between the language people used and their thought processes. In a book entitled *Frogs into Princes* (Real People Press, 1979), they published the results of their studies. They called their research Neuro-linguistic Programming (NLP).

NLP has been used extensively by psychologists and, more recently, by other disciplines, including sales. One noted discovery was that people gained access to information in one of three ways:

(a) Visual — with mental pictures

(b) Auditory — with sound

(c) Kinesthetic — with feeling

Put simply, the researchers found that some people reacted more strongly to visual stimuli — a picture, photograph, or illustration. Others reacted more strongly to auditory stimulation — a graphic description or detailed explanation of the subject. The third group relied on their feeling about a subject or situation. If they felt "good" or had

65

a "warm" feeling about something, then their reaction would be positive. If they felt "bad" or had "cold" feelings about the subject, then their reaction would be negative.

Most people respond in varying degrees to each of these stimuli, with one of them usually being dominant. To find out which mode is dominant for you, try the following simple experiment.*

Read the next line, close your eyes, and note your reaction.

THINK ABOUT YOUR FIRST CAR

What happened? Did you see the car's gleaming chrome, the glowing colors, and the glistening spokes?

Did you hear the roar of the muffler, or the scream of burning rubber, or the radio belting out the latest rock number?

Or did you once again experience that great feeling of owning your own set of wheels, of being independent, of appearing "cool" to your friends?

The chances are that you reacted in varying degrees to each of these stimuli but there was one that was much stronger than the others. If you're not sure, try the experiment again:

THINK ABOUT YOUR LAST BUSINESS MEETING
or
THINK ABOUT YOUR LAST HOLIDAY

You now know how you access information.

How do you translate this knowledge to the show floor and use it effectively? If you can quickly assess how each of your prospects accesses information, then you can readily develop a rapport that will make your task of gathering information that much easier.

---

* Reproduced with permission from the NLP Institute of Canada

We all have the ability to access information by all three modes, but, generally, one is better developed than the other two. Before looking at ways to discover a person's primary mode of access, make sure that you understand in detail how each of the modes operates.

(a) Visual: Visuals are those who understand what they see better than what they hear or feel. They take your words and translate them into meaningful pictures. Without those pictures, your words mean little to them. Even Einstein was a visual and, according to reports, he developed his famous Theory of Relativity by imagining himself riding invisible waves through the universe.

If you inhibit visual people from visualizing, they will not be able to understand. You will not have rapport and it is most unlikely that you will make the sale.

(b) Auditory: These people are influenced by sounds. They concentrate on things like voice inflections, rhythm, tone, pitch, and volume. These people buy when they interpret what they hear as being favorable and positive.

(c) Kinesthetic: This group is subject to deep feelings. They rely to a large extent on their "gut" feelings to help them decide on a course of action. If you are trying to sell them something, then first and foremost they must feel good about you, otherwise there will be no rapport and no sale.

Your purpose is to gather information to help you decide whether or not the person is a *Ready Buyer*. If you can find out how he or she accesses information, then it will help you develop a rapport and build trust. People don't buy words, they buy trust! Visuals trust more quickly by seeing pictures;

auditories build trust from hearing the right sounds; kinesthetic people trust their feelings.

Bandler and Grinder found many clues as to the way people accessed information. One of the most revealing was eye movement. They were able to closely relate eye movements to the individual's mode of access. Other clues were found in head movements, breathing changes, tonality changes, muscle tone, hand and arm positions, skin color, and the use of predicates. The way in which each of these clues relates to each mode can become a powerful tool in your sales arsenal. So, let's take a look at each one in turn:

1. How to recognize a visual

Visuals understand what they can see. External stimuli are interpreted as pictures in their minds that work like a silent movie — one frame at a time. As you talk to them, they see a series of pictures rolling past their mind's eye. Here's how you spot them. (Note: The following discussion on eye movement applies to right-handed people. Left-handed people will react exactly opposite.)

(a) Eye movements:

> *Up and to the left:* This eye movement tells you that they are seeing something in their past — they are reconstructing something that was triggered by your conversation. Now is a great time for you to say, "Tell me something about your office or factory," because they are remembering.

> *Up and to the right:* This movement tells you that they are constructing or creating a picture of the future. With this clue you might ask, "How do you see this fitting into your plans?"

(b) Head movements: For the visual, head movements tend to mirror their eye movements.

(c) Breathing changes: Visuals are generally shallow breathers and tend to stop breathing when they are accessing information. Since clothes tend to mask body movements, it is often difficult to recognize this clue in a visual. The easiest way is to watch their shoulders against a solid background.

(d) Tonality changes: Visuals can be spotted by their high-pitched or nasal tones.

(e) Tempo changes: Watch for quick bursts of words and a fast pace.

(f) Muscle tone changes: If you notice tension in the shoulders or abdomen, this is a clue that you are talking to a visual person.

(g) Hand and arm positions: Fingers are usually extended rather than clenched in a fist; arms are usually extended.

(g) Skin color changes: Some skin color changes can be subtle but observable to the alert salesperson. Visuals lose blood from their faces when accessing information, resulting in a slight paling.

(h) Predicates: These are the verbal clues to a person's access mode. Visuals use words like see, aim, bright, clear, dark, dull, foggy, hazy, hide, image, light, look, observe, oversight, pattern, picture, view, and vision. These are visual words that describe the pictures in the prospect's mind.

2. How to recognize an auditory

Auditories interpret ideas through sound. They develop trust in a person through the way in which things are said to them. In some cases, the way it is said is more important than what is said!

Everything you do with your voice helps the auditory person form an opinion.

(a) Eye movements: Auditories generally move their eyes from side to side. Sometimes these movements can be subtle so your powers of observation must be keen.

Left side: This movement suggests they are hearing past information. Try a question like this: "What did your partner say about the change?" If the eyes go to the left, the person is actually hearing the conversation he or she had about the change.

Right side: Movement to the right suggests construction. Try this test: ask, "What do you suppose people will say about this purchase?" If the eyes go to the right, the person is constructing a conversation that will happen in the future.

Down and to the left: When this happens, the auditory is usually involved in an internal dialogue. If you notice this behavior, it's a good time to stop talking and let the internal conversation run its course.

(b) Head movements: The auditory's head remains relatively level during conversation but moves from side to side in harmony with the eye movement.

(c) Breathing changes: A typical pattern is even breathing in the whole chest and diaphragm with prolonged exhalation.

(d) Tonality changes: The clue here is a clear, resonating tone.

(e) Tempo changes: Auditories talk in an even, rhythmic tempo.

(f) Muscle tone changes: Look for minor body rhythms and even body tension.

(g) Hand and arm positions: You'll receive a lot of hand and arm signals from auditories. Look for hands and arms folded, head tilted onto arms (the telephone position), hands touching mouth or chin, or counting with their fingers.

(h) Skin color changes: None that is noticeable.

(i) Predicates: Listen for the following words: argue, debate, discuss, hear, listen, loud, notice, quiet, ring, say, silent, sound, talk, tell, and verbalize. These are the kinds of words that describe an auditory's mental world.

3. How to recognize a kinesthetic

Kinesthetics are emotional people. They make their decisions based on how they feel about the person who is trying to communicate with them. They respond to hunches, gut feelings, instincts, and attitudes. Here's how they signal their mode of access:

(a) Eye movements:

Down and to the right: This indicates that the person is accessing information that is either tactile (relating to the touch), or visceral (gut). This is a good time to ask, "How do you feel about making this purchase?"

(b) Head movements: Follows same direction as the eyes.

(c) Breathing changes: Watch the stomach. Kinesthetics are generally deep breathers.

(d) Tonality changes: These people have low, deep-toned voices and except for the occasional outburst, their voices are more breathy.

(e) Tempo changes: Characterized by slow speech with long pauses.

(f) Muscle tone changes: Muscle movement indicates tactile accessing. An even relaxation of the muscles indicates some internal visceral accessing.

(g) Hand and arm positions: Look for upturned palms and bent arms.

(h) Skin color changes: Increased, fuller color is typical of a kinesthetic's face.

(i) Predicates: Look for feeling words such as cold, connect, feel, grasp, hard, hot, invite, link, rough, soft, solid, stiff, tender, touch, and warm.

Figure #3 should help you identify these different access modes. When the eyes move in the direction of the lines, they provide clues to the person's means of accessing information.

By identifying the type of person you are communicating with, you will be able to respond to them in a manner that they understand and appreciate. Selling is tough enough under normal circumstances. Why make it harder by saying to a kinesthetic, "Just picture this!" The person can't and won't picture what you're trying to get across, but they can feel it.

FIGURE #3
UNDERSTANDING EYE MOVEMENT

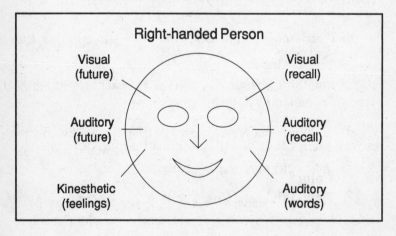

Eye accessing is an easy skill to practice. Virtually everyone you meet, whether at a show, at home, or in the office accesses information. Practice with everyone you meet until it becomes second nature to characterize a person according to his or her accessing mode, and to respond accordingly.

e. DRESS THE PART

As a smart salesperson you dress to suit your audience. You don't wear a dark business suit when calling on rural customers. You use that suit for calling on your business clients in their city offices.

The same rules apply to what you wear when exhibiting at trade and consumer shows. Wear what is appropriate to the audience and the nature of your exhibit. If you are demonstrating machinery, then you would want to wear a white smock or coveralls. At a woodworking show for the public, you could wear a woodworker's apron. If your product is chemicals, you might wear a white lab coat. However, for most trade shows, plain business attire is best. The trick is not to be overdressed or underdressed for the occasion. You want your prospects to feel comfortable when talking to you so that you can develop rapport and build trust.

It is also important for a prospect to be able to pick out booth staff from the crowd. Color-coded name tags help, but some companies go a step further by providing their booth staff with colored blazers, shirts, or sweaters.

When choosing the appropriate dress, considerations such as color, comfort, and style are all important.

1. Color

Prospects react strongly to color. It tends to have both physiological and psychological effects on people. The colors you select should lean more to the conservative than the theatrical; they should be easy to look at and inoffensive.

Studies have shown that the most popular color that meets these criteria is blue.

Colors should be chosen with your prospects in mind, not your own personal preferences.

Choosing the right outfit

2. Comfort

Don't try breaking in new shoes at a show; you and your productivity will most certainly suffer. Soft-bottom walking shoes can be both comfortable and stylish. Support stockings are helpful for men and women, relieving the strain of those long hours on hard floors.

3. Style

Once again, conservatism is best. In many situations business attire is preferable — but make sure it's fashionable. Choose materials that tell the prospect that you are a successful professional: avoid loud patterns.

In the business world your image is all important. Some salespeople look successful and seem to immediately engender trust in their clients. So, make sure that your wardrobe complements the image you wish to project. Not only should your clothes look comfortable and stylish, but you should also feel comfortable in them.

f. SUMMARY

In your search for the *Ready Buyer*, your approach to people will often mean the difference between success and failure. By mastering the techniques covered in this chapter, you should be able to quickly establish rapport with each prospect.

Prospecting is an important first ingredient in the total sales effort but there's still a long way to go before clinching a sale. In the next chapter we'll be looking at Boothmanship, which is the art of making your prospect welcome.

Sounds easy? Well, read on...maybe it's not as easy as you think!

8
BOOTHMANSHIP

Your behavior and the behavior of all of your colleagues staffing your booth at a show is of paramount importance. While an attractive booth may attract the interest of a visitor, it is the actions of the booth staff individually and as a group that determine whether or not the visitor stops for a closer look or just walks by.

This behavior is known as boothmanship and is governed by a definite set of rules.

a. RULES FOR THE SHOW

Shows can be stressful. Booth staff suffer both physically and psychologically from long show hours. To minimize the toll, there are some simple rules that should be followed.

1. Enjoy yourself

The first of these rules is to ENJOY YOURSELF, have some fun, put some sparkle into the serious business of selling. Shows can be exciting, they can be challenging, and they can generate enough business to keep you busy for a long time. So why not "lighten up" a bit! A little light-hearted banter will often help build rapport with a customer.

During a discussion on boothmanship at one of my group sessions, one of the participants commented on the fatigue he experienced at his shows. To overcome this fatigue, he tried "joking around" with his customers and found, much to his surprise, that his productivity increased noticeably. Being a very serious type, his attitude had obviously rubbed off on his visitors. My suggestion to him was that he should start off the day in a happy mood and not wait until he felt fatigued.

The lesson is clear. People love to deal with enthusiastic salespeople. Just think about some of your own shopping experiences and the salespeople you prefer to buy from.

Enthusiasm is contagious. The people you work with and the people you deal with will feel your enthusiasm and respond to it. It is a positive way of building rapport. So, don't hesitate to have fun at your next show. It will make life easier for you and your prospects.

2. Pace yourself

The second rule is to PACE YOURSELF. Shows can be grueling. Long hours on your feet, a lot of people to talk to, and a booth that must be attended at all times can be very demanding if you are not properly prepared to deal with the stresses.

As with many activities in life, there is a time to work, time to have fun, and time to rest. In order to perform at your peak, you must have the discipline to work hard, take adequate rest time, and have some fun as well.

Here are some rules that apply to pacing yourself at a show:

(a) Have a work schedule for your booth staff. The maximum shift length for efficient performance is four hours. The ideal time is two hours. A two-hour shift followed by a two-hour break seems to be the best arrangement for peak performance.

In some cases, long work days are unavoidable, particularly for smaller companies with limited staff. In this case, booth people should pace themselves and take breaks whenever possible.

(b) Arrive for your shift on time or preferably a few minutes early. Do this in fairness to your colleagues who are tired and need the break, and to your customers as well. They expect and deserve to meet staff who are enthusiastic and willing.

(c) When your shift is finished, get out of the booth. Put your feet up and relax. Take some fresh air — your body deserves it. Have a chat with fellow exhibitors who are taking breaks. Make the most of your time off so that you return refreshed and eager to sell.

(d) Don't party all night. Some people take advantage of being away from home to "Do the Town." This is fine after the show is over, but not during the show. Take an extra day or two to visit the local places of interest and enjoy the night life. It's a nice reward for a job well done.

While the show is on, don't engage in any after-hours activities that will impair your ability to perform the next day.

3. Behave yourself

Follow the rules of good business behavior and etiquette. Remember that you are the single most important ingredient in the success of your exhibit. Your mannerisms, behavior, appearance, and attitude will spell the difference between success and failure. Most of the do's and don'ts that follow are common sense, yet many salespeople seem to forget them when at a show. I see things that would never be done during a sales call with a client. Would you think of calling on a client with a hamburger in your hand? Of course not, yet here is an incident which parallels that kind of behavior.

It was a hardware show and everywhere the booths were crammed with visitors — except one. It was a prime location, at the end of an aisle, occupied by a major hardware distributor. Exposed as it was to three lanes of traffic, it should have been very busy, but there wasn't a single visitor at the booth.

Why?

The reason wasn't hard to see. The booth covered 1,500 square feet (approximately 135 m^2) and was loaded with products. In the middle of the booth was a large boardroom table, and sitting at this table were eight salespeople all eating lunch! The table was piled with fast food containers and the staff were busy shovelling it into their mouths. No wonder the visitors stayed away.

After the show, they had the nerve to complain that it was a poor show! For them, yes, but it was by their own doing. Other smarter and better-mannered exhibitors did well at the same show.

If you look around any trade show you will see salespeople sitting down reading the newspaper or a magazine, talking to friends or colleagues, or busy completing their company paperwork. These people will not be very successful at shows and a lot of them do not understand why.

I recall one trade show where two competitors were on adjacent aisles and had the same flow of traffic past their exhibits. One exhibitor sat behind a table with his assistant waiting for the customers to ask questions. Most walked by. The second exhibitor stood at the front of his exhibit and talked to people as they went by. When I talked to these exhibitors early in the afternoon (it was a one-day show), the first complained that he hadn't had a single lead and that the right people hadn't been invited to the show. I pointed out to him that his competitor, with similar products and the same traffic, was doing well and had a stack of leads. The first man still wasn't convinced, even though he could see his competitor and how he was selling!

Many visitors are shy or don't wish to commit themselves. If you appear to be busy or don't invite their comment with a well-chosen question, or make eye contact with them, they will walk by.

To be successful, you must "work the show." Good salespeople are always on their feet, looking for the *Ready Buyers* and presenting a pleasing, professional outlook to those passing the booth. They play by the commonsense rules that have been developed by successful exhibitors over many years.

Here is a list of do's and don'ts for all trade and consumer show exhibitors. Follow them carefully, and you will be one of the select group of peak performers.

b. SHOW DO'S

- *Know your products and services:* Take time before the show to thoroughly familiarize yourself with all of the products or services that you are selling. You will then be well prepared to answer most of the questions that arise during the show.

- *Be honest:* If you don't know the answer to a question, be honest about it. Don't try to con your prospect. Promise to get back to him or her right after the show. After all, it's another selling opportunity.

- *Know your booth:* Spend time learning all you can about your booth before the show starts. Know where everything is kept, how displays work, and how to arrange for show services if needed.

- *Know the show:* Be able to help out prospects with directions to washrooms, telephones, meeting rooms, exits, and eating areas.

- *Be well groomed:* Choose your attire carefully to suit your audience. This includes being freshly showered, clothes pressed, and hair neatly combed.

- *Be confident:* Confidence comes from being prepared. Follow the guidelines given in this book and you should feel confident to meet any eventuality, and that confidence will be felt by your visitors.

- *Keep your booth neat and attractive:* With crowds of people flowing through your booth, it needs constant attention and should always look as neat and tidy as it did when the show opened, right up to the closing bell.

- *Treat all visitors equally:* Everyone deserves your respect. Don't fall into the trap of making snap judgments about people. If you treat everyone the same, you may be surprised at where some of your future business comes from.

c. SHOW DON'TS

- *Don't smoke:* A lot of people find tobacco smoke annoying and some even find it repulsive. There is also a growing awareness of the dangers of second-hand smoke. So, don't take chances by smoking in your booth. If you can't wait four hours for a cigarette, try to arrange a two-hour shift. After smoking, be aware of the smell left on your breath and on your clothes. It may not be noticeable to you, but it is very noticeable to a non-smoker.

- *Don't sit:* Chairs in your booth are for visitors, not you. Don't sit down during your shift; be ready to greet visitors.

- *Don't drink:* This means any kind of beverage. Spilled coffee can be very damaging to your display. I recall one linen manufacturer who warned his people of the perils of drinking in his booth. Across the aisle was a coffee distributor who was giving away free samples. One of the booth staff took a free sample, which he set down on a display while talking to a prospect. Needless to say, it was knocked over with disastrous results. The manufacturer spent the rest of the day explaining to prospects that the linens they ordered would come without coffee stains!

- *Don't talk with colleagues:* People are reluctant to interrupt others. If you must have a conversation with a colleague, don't be so engrossed that you ignore a waiting prospect.

- *Don't leave your booth:* Prospects who have taken the time to visit your show deserve to have someone there to greet them when they show up.

- *Don't go into other booths unless you are invited:* This may be one of the written or unwritten rules of the show. In any case, you shouldn't take other exhibitors' time when the show is busy.

- *Don't knock the competition:* Never say negative things about your competition. People want to compare facts, not your opinions. By being positive about your competition, you create a positive atmosphere.

The above do's and don'ts are summarized below.

DO'S	DON'TS
Know your products and services	Smoke
Be honest if you don't know	Sit
Know your booth	Drink
Know the show	Talk with colleagues
Be well groomed	Leave your booth
Be confident	Visit other booths
Keep booth tidy	Knock the competition
Treat all visitors equally	

Follow these guidelines and you'll be among the top performers at any show.

d. CUSTOMER SERVICE

All efforts to get customers and prospects into your booth are to no avail if you don't service them properly once they are there. When the show is crowded and people are pushing, shoving, and waiting, it is all too easy to ignore a good prospect.

How often have you heard it said at a show, "It's too busy here now, let's come back later."

You've probably said it yourself, and how often did you go back? If it was a big show, you may even have forgotten where the booth was, or found something that interested you more.

Once a person enters your booth, they should receive some attention right away. Your attention to visitors will make the difference between so-so results and excellent results. Let's take a look at what constitutes good customer service at a show.

- *People waiting:* This happens when there are more visitors on the booth than there is staff to handle them. If you notice a person waiting, then you should at least acknowledge with a nod of the head or a smile. Better still, say something like, "I'll be with you in a minute." This lets the person know that he or she won't have to wait too long and that you value that person's presence.

- *Who sits down:* Chairs are for visitors. An exhausted visitor will appreciate an invitation to sit down for a moment while waiting for your attention or listening to your presentation. Be aware of the signs of fatigue and use it to your advantage by offering a chair to the tired visitor.

- *Refreshments:* If you do provide some form of refreshment, be a gracious host and make sure that it is offered to everyone who visits you. Some companies hire a host whose job it is to make sure that visitors are taken care of while waiting for a salesperson to help them.

- *Keep your promises:* Promises made to customers are important, whether you make them at a show or elsewhere. Keep careful notes of your conversations with prospects and make sure that any promises made are taken care of immediately after the show. A good place to make notes is on the lead card, which is described in chapter 10.

- *The golden rule:* Do unto others as you would have them do unto you if you were in their place. Think of the kinds of service that makes your blood boil. Then think of the kind of service that pleases you. Make sure that your service pleases your customers in the same way that you like to be treated. You can't be too helpful.

9

MAKING THE PROPER APPROACH

Approaching prospects seems to be a major stumbling block for many booth personnel. Some feel inhibited, others feel that they may be too pushy, but most simply don't know how to do it.

The proper approach is designed to accomplish a number of things. First, it will give some indication of the prospect's interest in your product or service. Second, it will give you a clue to the prospect's mode of accessing information: whether the person is visual, auditory, or kinesthetic (see chapter 7). Third, it is a starting point for the process of qualifying the prospect (see chapter 10).

As I walk around shows, I see many salespeople wasting valuable opportunities by making the wrong approach. Many begin with the most commonly used question in sales:

"May I help you?"

We all know the answer to this question: "No thanks, just looking."

If we know the answer, why bother asking in the first place?

Here are a few more non-starters:

"How are you doing today?" Answer: "Fine, thanks."

"Nice day, isn't it?" Answer: "Yes, great."

"How are you enjoying the show?" Answer: "So far, so good."

Eye contact is another tool that can be badly misused. While walking through a show recently, I noticed a salesperson staring directly at me, trying to make eye contact. He was standing at the side of a double booth, beside a display unit. While walking past, I decided to see what action he would take if I failed to acknowledge his eye contact.

Walking exceptionally slowly, I studied his display and murmured appreciative noises to myself. The salesperson didn't respond, he just kept staring at me, waiting to make eye contact. I purposely ignored his stare while watching him through peripheral vision. As I approached the end of the booth where he was standing, my patience ran out and I looked him squarely in the eye. No greater eye contact was ever made.

What did he do? He smiled and said to me, "Nice day, isn't it?" To which I answered, "Yes," and kept walking.

What a waste of a valuable sales opportunity. All that was needed was a statement to get me talking and thinking. After that, things would have been easy.

The goal in your approach is to begin qualifying the visitor immediately. Therefore, you want to make an opening that will get him or her talking about business.

Try this one next time someone walks past your booth: "I noticed from your badge that you are a printer. How do you handle down time?"

This type of question will get the person thinking and talking about his or her business. While the person is talking, you can be watching and listening for clues to the dominant mode of accessing information and starting to qualify him or her.

Demonstrations make it easier to approach people. While the demonstration is going on, watch the crowd carefully. Pick out those who show above average interest and talk to them. Since you won't have time to talk to everyone in the crowd, this makes the most effective use of your time.

How do you pick out those with above-average interest? By watching their body signals. They are watching intently and probably leaning forward, at the same time ignoring all outside influences that might otherwise distract them. Good people watchers can develop a sixth sense about the members of an audience. If you watch the crowds carefully, you should be able to sort the serious ones from those "just looking."

Once the demonstration is finished, you should be standing next to the person you have picked out, ready to approach them with the question: "What part of the demonstration did you find most helpful?" A simple question that gets the person talking and thinking.

Creating opening lines is not difficult. Hold brainstorming sessions with your colleagues before the show. Try to come up with all possible situations and find suitable opening lines. Remember to ask questions that demand thought on the part of the prospect and cannot be passed off with a non-committal answer as he or she walks by.

As you will see in the next chapter, you have only a few precious moments to find out if you are talking to the right person, so you can't afford to waste a second. A good approach puts you well on the road to success.

10

QUALIFYING YOUR PROSPECTS

Time, at a busy show, is a scarce resource. You have just a few days to gather all those leads you have planned to collect and you're going to have to work very hard to get them. Your job is to quickly qualify each person that you talk to and decide on the spot whether you should spend more of your valuable time in a presentation.

In many respects, your approach to the customer can be likened to that of other professionals such as doctors and lawyers. When you go to see your doctor, the first thing he or she does is to qualify you. A doctor wants to know why you have come and what your symptoms are before deciding on a course of action. Similarly, a lawyer will question you carefully before making a recommendation to you. As a sales professional, you must do the same.

a. "TIRE KICKER" OR PROSPECT?

You, through experience and hard work, must learn how to qualify a visitor before spending valuable time with the "tire kickers." The process of qualifying is one of the most important things that you have to do and the techniques should be well rehearsed. You should be able to qualify anyone in four minutes or less. That adds up to 15 per hour — about the maximum a good salesperson can deal with.

Your approach to your visitor (as discussed in the previous chapter) will have got you off to a good start. By now, you should know the type of business the person is engaged in, how he or she accesses information, and what he or she is looking for. If, after getting this information, you decide the visitor is a prospect, then you have good basic information that will help you start the qualifying process. However, no action should be taken unless you are *convinced* that this visitor has potential as a prospect. If you have doubts, politely close the interview and move on.

b. QUALIFYING

The process of qualifying can be divided into six components. If the person fails any one of the six tests, you should stop qualifying immediately and move on to the next. Do not, however, discard these visitors completely. Make sure that you have their names and addresses — they may be good long-term prospects and worth putting on your follow-up lists.

Qualifying your prospect

The following six attributes will help tell you which prospects require further testing and which ones don't. The acronym **ACTION** will help you remember the attributes.

1. **A**uthority
2. **C**ash
3. **T**ime
4. **I**dentity
5. **O**perational constraints
6. **N**eed

You don't have to test for these attributes in this order. After reviewing the next few pages, decide on a qualifying patter that works for you. Remember — don't take ACTION with anyone unless they qualify.

1. Authority

It is important to find out early on whether your prospect has buying authority or is a buying influence. Knowing this will tell you how to slant your questions and information.

How do you determine authority? Job titles on name badges may be of some help but are often misleading. Not all buyers have buying authority and neither do all vice-presidents. The only way to be sure is to ask.

Don't be afraid to ask — it doesn't have to be difficult or unfriendly. In fact, the simpler you keep it, the better. It makes you sound less formal and more friendly — essential ingredients to building the rapport you are seeking.

Questions should be structured to suit the person you are talking to. Here are some examples:

- *For the visual:*
  "How is your decision making structured?"
  "Do you see anyone else in your company involved in making this decision?"

- *For the auditory:*
  "Tell me a little about your company. How does the decision making take place?"
  "Is there anyone else who should be involved in our discussions about your manufacturing needs?"

- *For the kinesthetic:*
  "Is there anyone else you should connect with on this decision?"
  "Are there others you want to be in touch with?"

Each question is aimed at the individual and is created to complement his or her own accessing system.

2. Cash

Here we are talking about financial resources — can the prospect afford your product, or is it just a dream? The other side of this coin is — can you afford to do business with him or her?

Many of us dream or fantasize about things we would like to own both personally and professionally. Listen carefully to what the prospect is saying and you can tell whether the proposed purchase is a reality or just a dream.

The prospect might say, "That press is just what we need, as soon as we're big enough...."

There's no need to listen any further — it's just a dream. This person might be a good long-term prospect, but is not a *Ready Buyer*.

Trying to find out whether a prospect can afford your product is easier said than done, and you have, at most, only a couple of minutes left in your four-minute quest. You would like to say, "Come on, can you really afford this thing, or are we just spinning our wheels?" While this is obviously too direct, there are other ways of asking the same question. Here are a few:

- *For the visual:*
  "What kinds of equipment do you now have in your factory?"
  "What does your budget look like for this kind of purchase?"

- *For the auditory:*
  "Tell me how you prefer to acquire major equipment, buying or leasing?"
  "It sounds as if you have an "open to buy" in the fall.

- *For the kinesthetic:*
  "Do you have a fixed budget for this purpose?"
  "Do you have a rough estimate of how much you would like to spend on this purchase?"

Each of the above questions was framed to gently find out something about the prospect's resources.

Some other areas you might want to inquire about are other suppliers, customers, length of time in business, number of employees, and company ownership.

3. Time

Time is of the essence. You are searching for the *Ready Buyer* who will buy within the period that you have defined for your own business (see chapter 7). If your prospect isn't ready to buy within that period, then don't waste any more valuable time. Put the person on your follow-up list and move on to the next prospect. Here's an example:

Someone might say, "That's the most incredible thing. It's going to be perfect in our operation; the price seems good and I like the color!"

"Great!" you reply. "When are you planning to make this purchase?"

"We should look at buying one as soon as our new plant is completed."

"Oh, and when will that be?" you ask.

"Well, we haven't actually started yet, but we're hoping for early next year."

Oops! You came close, but you don't have a *Ready Buyer* here. This is a good long-term prospect, but not for today.

The reality of the situation is that once the new plant is built, which might be a year or two away, your product will need a new presentation to this customer. In addition, there will be all sorts of product improvements as well as new competition. So if this is a future prospect, why waste time at the show? Save your energy for those who are ready to buy NOW.

Here's how you can ask about time:

- *For the visual:*
  "When do you see this purchase being made?"
  "It looks like you're about ready now?"

- *For the auditory:*
  "Tell me about your timing for this type of purchase."
  "It sounds like the kind of purchase that you are prepared to make now."

- *For the kinesthetic:*
  "Do you have a grasp of your timing?"
  "I want to get a solid understanding of your timing."

4. Identity

It is important that you have an organized way of recording the identity of each prospect. The method you choose depends to some extent on the system of visitor registration used by the show manager.

(a) Computerized identification

Many of the more sophisticated systems use computers to capture the basic information about each visitor. This information is usually generated from registration cards and pre-registration information completed by each visitor.

- *Embossed plastic badges:* Similar to credit cards, these badges usually carry the name, company, and address of the visitor and are worn in a transparent plastic badgeholder. An exhibitor who wishes to record a person's name removes the badge from its holder, places a special multi-part form supplied by the show manager in an imprinter, and records the basic information.

  These machines may be rented by exhibitors from show managers. The forms have spaces for writing comments or instructions for follow up. The badge is then returned to the visitor for use at other booths.

- *Coded badges:* Here the computer generates a thin cardboard badge bearing the basic information plus a code of some kind. The code may be numerical or alpha-numerical and is exclusive to each visitor. Exhibitors are provided with special forms with provision for the code number and a number of other pre-coded requests such as send literature, etc. When using the forms, exhibitors need only record the visitor's code number, plus any special request code numbers and any comments they wish to make. The forms are returned to the show office and a print-out of all leads with mailing labels and information requested is provided usually within 24 or 48 hours.

(b) Manual identification

- *Typewritten badges:* With this form of registration, lead forms must be filled out by hand. In these cases you can often speed things up by stapling the prospect's business card to the lead form, leaving only comments or requests to be written in by hand.

- *Lead forms:* These are sometimes provided by show management. If you have to design your own, keep it simple. You will find the acronym **ACTION** —

Authority, Cash, Time, Identity, Operational constraints, and Need — a useful guide to the kinds of information you will need to collect. Remember, you won't have time to fill in a lot of details. Make your notes readable and understandable, but use point form to speed up the process.

You should leave space on the card for checking off requests for literature and catalogues and any other requirements peculiar to your operation. Also leave room for any additional notes you feel necessary. Printing on the lead card a list of the items you have on display can save you time, too. As you talk to the prospect, you can check off those items of interest to him or her. Worksheet #3 is an example of a lead form.

5. Operational constraints

You should be aware of the potential constraints to your doing business. If you are dealing with government departments or some large corporations, regulations may require certain types of purchases to go out to tender. Find this out early so that you can ask questions about tendering criteria and how to get on the bid list.

Another constraint is the applicability of your product in certain business, political, or natural environments. Sometimes there is no fit because of size, number of employees, export quotas, type of business, etc. Your job is to uncover these constraints early to avoid problems or misunderstandings later.

Here are the kinds of questions you might ask:

• *For the visual:*
"Tell me what your manufacturing process looks like."
"Let me see if I understand...."

95

WORKSHEET #3
LEAD FORM

Name of Show_____**Date** _____

Is Prospect a Buying **A**uthority?_____

Does prospect have the **C**ash?_____

Will prospect buy within **T**ime period?_____

Identity: Name_____

Title_____

Company_____

City_____

Province/State_____Postal/Zip code_____

Telephone (   )_____Fax (   )_____

Operational constraints_____

Need_____

Appointment made_____

Service offered_____

Other comments _____

_____

_____

_____

_____

_____

- *For the auditory:*
"It sounds as though you are planning to go to tender. Is that right?"
"Tell me if I heard you correctly ...."

- *For the kinesthetic:*
"Can you put your finger on the problem?"
"I'd like to develop a solid understanding of your manufacturing process."

Save time and grief by finding out about operational constraints up front.

6. Need

Need should be the first thing you establish. Remember the salesperson in chapter 7? He spent valuable time telling me all about his boats, but failed to ask me whether I needed one. A simple question would have saved him a lot of energy and help maintain his performance throughout the show.

Need is the basis for any sales.

No need...no sale!

When we train salespeople in the field, we stress the value of working with prospects to uncover their needs. Often, initial negative responses can be turned into firm orders by exploring with your prospects how your products or services can be of help to them.

Although this method works well in the field, it is not appropriate for a show where time is limited. Each minute that you spend with an unqualified prospect may mean that as many as 15 or 20 people have passed by your booth (see chapter 7) and among them there may have been a *Ready Buyer*.

You can easily establish need by asking a few simple questions. In the case of our boat salesperson, he could have asked, "Are you looking for a new boat?" I would have told him, "No!" and he could have moved on to other prospects.

Here are some other suggestions that will help you uncover needs:

- *For the visual:*
  "What are you looking for?"
  "Can you picture this in your office?"

- *For the auditory:*
  "Does this ring any bells for you?"
  "Did something click when you saw our product?"

- *For the kinesthetic:*
  "I have a feeling we have the product you need."
  "How does this product fit with your needs?"

If your prospect passes all of these tests — congratulations — you have found the person we have been looking for...a *Ready Buyer*. Now you are ready to take **ACTION** and move to the next step.

11

MAKING YOUR PRESENTATION

Once you have found your *Ready Buyer*, you have to decide on the course of action most appropriate to the circumstances. For most products or services, a presentation of some kind is in order. The timing, length, and completeness of the presentation must be decided by you.

You might choose to make a full presentation on the spot, give a quick summary of your product or service with a request for an appointment at a later date, or make an appointment for a convenient time after the show at your prospect's or your place of business.

a. REVIEW YOUR GOALS

To help you make that decision, review your goals. If your goal is to make sales at the show, then a complete demonstration or presentation on the spot is in order. Bear in mind that this will reduce the number of contacts that you can make during your shift and should be reflected in your planning and staffing schedule.

If your goal is something other than a sale, then you might question the validity of a full presentation. Perhaps you can whet the prospect's appetite by presenting a few benefits and getting him or her to commit to a future appointment for a full presentation — perhaps with technical staff present. Whatever you do, don't oversell at this stage. Watch the prospect's body language and close off as soon as you see your objective is attained.

Regularly scheduled group presentations, often conducted by experts from the factory or laboratory, are appropriate for those you qualify as *Ready Buyers*. Invite them to sit in on the next group presentation. Don't expect your prospects to wait more than a few minutes for the next session, however. The bonus to this arrangement is that it frees you to concentrate on screening and qualifying other prospects.

The Ready Buyer

b. THE PRESENTATION

The presentation comes at an important stage in your interaction with your prospects. They stopped by because they remembered your show promotion, or they heard about your product from another source, or something on your display attracted their attention. So far they have been subjected to several minutes of questioning by you, and have not had their basic curiosity satisfied. On the other hand, you know quite a bit about them.

Now it's time to satisfy their curiosity.

1.   The opening

At the beginning of your presentation, you should let the prospect know what you are doing. The simple transition from information getter to information giver is easily made with a question such as, "Can I show you how our widgets work?"

Another way to make the transition is to summarize the information you have gleaned from the prospect during the qualifying process. You could say, for example, "So, if I understand you correctly, you are looking for high quality parts that are cost effective in manufacturing and dependable in the field, and you need them immediately. Is that correct?"

This helps develop a commitment from the prospect and move you closer to achieving your goal.

2.   The body of the presentation

The body of the presentation must create excitement and desire in the mind of your prospect.

To do this, make use of what you have learned about your prospect already by talking in language he or she understands. Enhance this by talking about your products or services in terms of features and benefits. You can talk all you want about the bells and whistles on your product but unless you relate them to benefits for the user, the prospect won't really care about them at all. In fact, he or she may not even understand them.

Unless you answer the question "What will it do for me?" you won't make a sale, no matter how much you talk.

Here's a good example of how not to do it, as experienced by me when I first set out to buy a personal computer.

Not knowing anything about computers, I decided to look around and ask questions. The first place I headed for was a large computer store where I explained my situation to the salesperson who greeted me. The salesperson immediately launched into a long discussion of operating systems and memory capacities that went completely over my head. The salesperson called the system he was extolling "user friendly," but there was nothing friendly about it to me. I left the store completely mystified and confused.

Over the next 18 months, I ventured into different stores, each time experiencing the same jargon-loaded presentation, until finally I found someone willing to talk to me in language I understood. I now have a "friendly" computer consultant and a "friendly" computer system, but it took me, as a *Ready Buyer*, over 18 months to find a "customer friendly" salesperson!

At a show, you don't have even 18 minutes to sell. Your job is to tell your prospects what your product or service will do for them in a language they can understand — and that is the language of benefits.

3. Features and benefits

Features are the physical characteristics of the product or service. In order to excite your prospect, you must also sell the benefits that go with the features, otherwise you're liable to get a ho-hum reaction.

Imagine, for example, that you are selling a line of coffee cups. The features of this cup are shape, material, design, a hole in the top, and a handle.

"So what!" your customer says, "What's so special about them? I've seen a million more like 'em."

Features are "so what" statements. *A good benefit statement tells simply and clearly what a particular feature will do for the prospect.*

"Yes, but this cup has a well-balanced handle which makes it easier to hold when full, and it is insulated so that your coffee stays hot longer."

"Hey, that's just what I've been looking for!" exclaims the customer, and you've made your sale.

Here are two more examples:

Feature: My personal computer has a hard disk.

Benefits: Faster access to your programs and files, no need to keep changing diskettes.

Feature: My bank offers overdraft protection.

Benefits: Avoids embarrassment of bounced checks if you accidentally overdraw your account, preserves your credit rating, avoids charges applied to bounced checks.

Think, for a moment, about one of your own products. How many features does it have? Probably quite a few. And what are the benefits that go with each of those features?

This is an exercise that all salespeople should do with all of their products, particularly prior to a show. By writing down the features and benefits, it will help fix them in your mind.

Another worthwhile exercise is to do the same thing for your competitor's products, from a customer's point of view. When you are faced with an objection from a prospect as he or she compares your product with your competitor's down the aisle, you'll be in good position to handle the objection.

Take a moment to fill out Worksheet #4. List five features and benefits for one of your products and do the same for a similar product sold by your nearest competitor. (While space is allowed for five features and benefits, you should list as many as you can think of.)

WORKSHEET #4
FEATURES AND BENEFITS

FEATURES	BENEFITS
My product	
1. _____	_____
2. _____	_____
3. _____	_____
4. _____	_____
5. _____	_____
My competitor's product:	
1. _____	_____
2. _____	_____
3. _____	_____
4. _____	_____
5. _____	_____

If you're not sure about your competition, shows are good places to find out

It is worthwhile repeating this exercise for each product or service you have so that you are prepared for the inevitable comparisons.

4. Getting feedback

Even though you may have a dozen benefits lined up, it doesn't follow that your prospects will be excited by all of them. Your job then, is to find out which benefits strike a favorable note with your current prospects and to concentrate on those.

Don't fall into the trap of telling prospects all about your product without getting some feedback. You could be spinning your wheels and wasting time. A good way to start is by asking a simple question like, "What are you looking for in a coffee cup?"

This should bring a specific answer such as, "Well, I need a cup that's good looking and not expensive."

With this simple question you have identified two areas of need...appearance and cost. However, before addressing these needs, you should explore further to see if the prospect has any other needs. You can do this by acknowledging the first two needs and asking a further simple question such as:

- *For the visual:* "You want a coffee cup that is not only attractive but inexpensive, is there anything else that you are looking for in a cup?"

- *For the auditory:* "Tell me what else it should have."

- *For the kinesthetic:* "What else do you feel is important in a cup?"

Once you have the complete set of needs, you can treat each one individually, matching benefits to need and explaining them fully. Make sure that your prospect understands how each benefit matches each of the needs that have been identified by continuing to ask questions as you proceed. For example, you might say, "Let's deal with cost first. Our cups are made of a new, improved material that allows us to compete very favorably with the imports now flooding the market. How does that look (sound, feel) to you?"

5. Getting them involved

During the presentation, it is helpful to get your prospects involved with as many senses as possible. You are already using their accessing modes to involve their thinking processes.

For visuals, you can expand by painting graphic word pictures. The sound of machines, people talking, or the sounds of production will impress the auditories. For the kinesthetic, let them handle the product, push buttons, or play with it.

If possible, have samples available. People come to shows to experience things and this is best accomplished by letting them see, hear, and feel our products. If they can have a sample, so much the better. If a picture is worth 1,000 words, then a sample is worth 10,000.

6. Technical information

Where technical questions are likely to be asked, you should have good back-up material available. While it is not necessary for you to be able to answer every question yourself, it is important that you know where to find the information. This can be provided in a variety of ways. You may have on-site specifications and catalogues, an on-site expert, or a hot line back to the plant or laboratory with the assurance that there will be someone there to give you a speedy answer. If the question cannot be answered on the spot, it should be followed up as soon as possible after the show.

Quick and efficient access to information is most important. It will save you time and energy and, more important, it will impress your prospect with the professional caliber of your operation.

7. Handling objections

An objection is a negative comment about your product. It's the thing that many inexperienced salespeople fear, but what seasoned professionals look forward to because they know that when an objection is skillfully handled, a sale is within sight.

Often, an objection is the prospect's way of telling you that they have an unsatisfied need.

106

When you hear an objection, the first rule is *stay calm*. Dealing with objections requires that you be well prepared beforehand. Have a bull session with your colleagues before the show, with some playing devil's advocate and raising all the objections they can think of. In this way, you'll hone your skills and be able to calmly handle all objections that come along.

The first reaction to an objection should simply be to ask the prospect if there is anything else that he or she hasn't told you. "So you are concerned about the price. Is there anything else that concerns you?" This way you get all the problems out in the open quickly so you can deal with them one by one.

Here's another approach: "You're concerned that our product seems too expensive. May I ask what you are comparing us to?"

Once you have this information, you can go to work. If you've done your homework and know the benefits of your competitor's product, you can answer something like this:

"You said you were concerned about extended warranties. Does ABC company offer the warranty you're looking for?" (You know they don't, having done your homework.)

If it looks as though the objection will take a long time to deal with, it may be better to put it off until after the show. "Mr. Prospect, you've brought up a good point and I'd like to show you in detail how our machine can overcome the problem you mentioned. In order to do that I need to spend some time with you when we can both relax and examine this thoroughly. I would like to come to your office next week to explain everything. What would be a good day for you, Tuesday or Wednesday?"

8. Buying signals

Buying signals are words or actions that tell us that the prospect is ready to say "Yes!" These signals are often subtle and easily overlooked. It is crucial to recognize these signals so that you do not prolong the presentation once the prospect has decided to buy.

As soon as you start talking benefits, you should be on the alert for buying signals, even while handling objections. The signals may be verbal or non-verbal.

Here are some verbal signals: "Interesting." "Looks good." "Nice feel to it." "Does it come in other colors?" "What is your shipping policy?"

These phrases tell you that the prospect has started to think about using the product and has accepted the purchase. You may even hear some overtones of possessiveness in the voice or choice of words. Stay alert and listen closely.

Some of the non-verbal signals are easier to spot. Watch for the moment when the prospect takes a step closer, picks up the sample, and examines it closely. Another signal is the nodding of the head and the dilation of the pupils.

When you get a buying signal, deal with it immediately. Don't talk yourself out of a sale. Close!

9. The close

This is the culmination of all that has gone before. Let's quickly review the steps that have led to the current position:

(a) You established contact and communication with the prospect.

(b) You qualified the prospect using the **ACTION** formula.

(c) You established a list of needs.

(d) You matched the benefits of your product to each of the prospect's needs.

(e) You made sure that your prospect fully understood and agreed on how each benefit satisfied his or her buying need.

As you proceed through stages (d) and (e) above, you should be constantly on the lookout for buying signals. There is no need to laboriously work through all the needs if you get a buying signal early.

Only deal with one need at a time. As you do this, one of three things can happen:

(a) The prospect agrees that he or she understands the benefit you have described, at which point you move on to the next benefit.

(b) The prospect raises an objection which you must deal with in the manner described above.

(c) You receive a buying signal, at which point you ask for the commitment that will satisfy your show goals.

You are now ready to close.

12

CLOSING THE SALE

The last chapter touched briefly on the final stage in the sales process — closing. This chapter looks at the six golden rules for closing:

(a) If you don't ask...you won't get the order.

(b) Before you ask, make sure you know what you're asking for.

(c) It's better to be a little early than a whole lot late.

(d) Always have a back-up goal.

(e) Always get a commitment.

(f) Make a statement the prospect will remember you by.

If the first stages in the selling process have been followed correctly, then closing should be the natural final step. Unfortunately, for many, this is where the sale is lost. I have seen willing customers actually talked out of buying by a salesperson who didn't know when to stop talking. Instead of writing the order and thanking the customer for the business, the salesperson continued to present the product, annoying the customer who became too impatient to buy. The sale was lost.

Some salespeople hesitate to close because they fear a negative reply — they hate to hear that big-little word...NO! To them, this response means that the prospect hasn't liked what they've said and is rejecting their ideas, and indirectly them. That's a pretty heavy burden.

On the other hand, the successful salesperson has learned that a negative answer means other things, such as:

"You haven't given me enough information to decide."

"You didn't listen to what I told you earlier, and you haven't cleared up my objections."

"I'm not interested now but I will be interested tomorrow."

"I never say yes the first time...Ask me again."

Whatever the true motive behind the negative answer, the experienced salesperson knows not to take it personally. It presents a personal challenge to find the true cause of the negative answer and do something about it. That's what selling is all about.

So, if you view closing as an act of confirming with your prospect that you are on the right track, the burden disappears and you can close with confidence.

a. IF YOU DON'T ASK...YOU WON'T GET THE ORDER

Of course, at a show, as we've said before, time is of the essence and you can't wait too long to close a sale. Each minute you spend talking to a prospect who will not buy is a waste of valuable time during which some 15 to 20 other prospects have passed by your booth.

Another common scenario is that of the salesperson determined to give a complete presentation regardless of the buying signals being transmitted by the prospect.

Here's a good example of this scenario that I happened to overhear at a recent show. The salesperson qualified the prospect well and began his presentation. After a while, the prospect said, "This is the first time I've seen your product and I'm impressed."

"Thank you," the salesperson said, "but don't let me forget to tell you about the warranty that comes with each purchase." Whereupon, he launched into a detailed description of his warranty package.

"Well, I'm convinced," the prospect interjected.

"Good, it's also important to understand the packaging of this item which has been designed to...."

Finally, the prospect insisted, "How do I order some?"

At this point the salesperson finally got the message and pulled out his order pad.

If you had spoken to this salesperson afterward, he would have insisted that he had closed the sale. He would not have acknowledged that it was, in reality, the customer who had closed the sale. By his insensitivity, this salesperson not only risked losing a sale, but also wasted valuable time that could have resulted in additional sales to other prospects.

b. BEFORE YOU ASK, MAKE SURE YOU KNOW WHAT YOU'RE ASKING FOR

This rule refers back to the discussion in chapter 2 of setting goals for the show. You should refer to the primary goal you set for the show and base your closing strategy on reaching that goal.

If your goal was —

(a) to make sales...ask for the order,

(b) to get qualified leads...ask for information, or

(c) to set up appointments...ask for the appointment.

The most common goal is to make sales. Let's take this goal and review a few closing lines that work:

- *For the visual:*
  "Would you like to see this delivered by the end of the week?"
  "It looks like we've got what you need."
  "Can you picture your results with our new process?"

- *For the auditory:*
  "It sounds like we've got the solution for you."
  "Does that ring any bells for you?"
  "Something tells me that this is the right product for you."

- *For the kinesthetic:*
  "I have a feeling that we've got a good fit here."
  "Do you have a firm grasp on the benefits of this installation?"
  "It all boils down to one simple answer, Yes or No."

What if you misinterpret the buying signals and try to close too early?

This is a real concern and often a cause for holding back. It shouldn't be, as you'll learn from third rule of closing.

c. IT'S BETTER TO BE A LITTLE EARLY THAN A WHOLE LOT LATE

The trick here is to find the balance between being too pushy and being assertive by asking for what you want. Mastery of this technique comes with experience. Seasoned professionals learn to sense when their prospects are ready to buy; they instinctively recognize the signals and ask for the close. They weren't born with this skill but learned it in the school of hard knocks where trial and error is the teacher.

To develop a sense of timing, you must try and try again. Don't be scared of making a mistake — you can usually work your way out of it if you don't panic. Here's an example:

113

"So, Mr. Prospect, it sounds as if this is the product for you?"

"Not so fast! I'm not ready to buy from you, or anyone else, yet."

"Oh! Is there something else you would like this product to do?"

You see, it's quite easy to turn a negative response into an opportunity to uncover more information. With this new information, you are better armed to move the prospect closer to closing.

So far, we've assumed that your prospect will fall in line with the goal you have set for your company and yourself. For instance, you may have a company goal of $20,000 in sales, which breaks down into a personal goal for each salesperson of $5,000 for the show (or 20 sales of $250 each). This may be a good goal for the type of product or service that you are selling, but what if it doesn't fit in with the prospect's requirements? Suppose the prospect says:

"Yes, it's the kind of merchandise I think will work in my store, but I'd like to sample it first with a smaller order of $100, and see how it works out."

d. ALWAYS HAVE A BACK-UP GOAL

In the above case, unless you have a minimum order requirement or some other constraint, you accept the order even though it falls short of your personal goal. The successful salesperson always has a fall-back position in case the original goal cannot be met.

The fall-back position in the above case was a lower dollar amount. Other positions you may choose could be an alternative appointment date, an introduction to the person with real buying authority, a testimonial, another call...and so on.

e. ALWAYS GET A COMMITMENT

Whether you meet your original goal or have to take a fall-back position, this is the one final closing rule that should always be followed.

Don't be caught off guard if your original goal is unattainable. Always get a commitment in some form from the prospect before ending the presentation. Having qualified the prospect as a *Ready Buyer*, made your full presentation, and answered objections, you must strive to get a commitment, otherwise your effort will have been wasted. If you can't make a sale today, make a follow-up appointment, confirm it, and make the sale tomorrow.

f. MAKE A STATEMENT THE PROSPECT WILL REMEMBER YOU BY

You have taken the current prospect as far as you can at the show and you must now end your conversation with something that he or she will remember you by. The prospect has given you a commitment to do or buy something. Now one last statement is required from you to round out your conversation and leave the prospect with a good feeling about you and your company. This is Golden Rule #6.

This last statement is really the icing on the cake. It's something extra that you can do to solidify the rapport that you have built up during your 10- to 15-minute conversation. Before the prospect leaves, you should say:

"I'm looking forward to our meeting on the fourteenth."

"I'm anxious to hear your feedback."

"I know you will feel good about this decision."

Your closing statement should be honest and sincere — a little something to show your prospects that you really do care. If you are not looking forward to seeing them on the fourteenth, then don't say it. If you really mean it and are sincere, then let them know. Remember that you are dealing

115

with people. While your customers may become statistics at the end of the show when you report your results, they must be more than that to you.

When you take the time to build rapport and help your customer make an intelligent buying decision, you are taking an important step in creating a successful business relationship. You can spend a lot of post-show time developing this relationship. It can bring repeat business, valuable referrals, and a great sense of achievement.

With your goals met, the show is over — but you still have work to do.

PART III
AFTER THE SHOW

13

FOLLOW-UP IS THE PAYOFF

If you collected a thousand leads at a show and didn't follow up on them, what use would they be? None at all. In fact, your months of effort in planning, attending, qualifying, and collecting those leads would have been wasted. Yet many companies do a poor job of following up the leads they collect at shows.

An effective follow-up system should be as carefully planned as the rest of your show activities — and should be done at the same time. When you know that you have a good follow-up system in place, then your qualifying and lead-collecting activities at the show take on far more meaning and urgency.

Another important consideration is your potential customers. Put yourself in their place. If you properly qualified the person as a *Ready Buyer*, gave a full sales presentation, and sent the person away with a promise to make contact after the show, you probably created considerable excitement and expectation in his or her mind. What's more, the customer probably spent time comparing your products with those of your competitors and left the show with a good idea of what he or she wanted to buy.

In order to clinch this sale, you must follow-up immediately while the excitement is still alive and before your competitors grab the order.

If you wait more than a week, the chances are that the prospect will have cooled off and may have placed the order elsewhere.

If you wait more than 30 days, you might as well throw the leads in the garbage.

Time is of the essence in any lead follow-up program. You must have a plan that allows you to contact all leads in some manner, as quickly as possible.

The following six points are the elements of a good lead follow-up program:

(a) Set a realistic goal for the number of leads you plan to collect during the show (see chapter 2).

(b) Design or use a lead-collecting system that makes recording and retrieval easy. If large numbers are expected, make sure that the system will generate mailing labels without a lot of extra effort.

(c) Plan your lead follow-up system well ahead of the show and have it ready to roll immediately after the show (see discussion of methods that follows).

(d) Set deadlines for all follow-up activities and brief all staff on the importance of meeting deadlines and their individual roles in the project.

(e) Set up a system to record and review results of your follow-up program.

(f) Set a date for the final review.

There are three methods of follow-up: direct mail, telemarketing, and personal sales calls.

Many companies use more than one method. What you use will depend on your market, the number of leads you collected, and the promises made by your staff during the show. Let's take a more detailed look at the role that each of these methods can play in your follow-up activities.

a. DIRECT MAIL

If you receive a large number of leads, direct mail offers the quickest way of getting in touch with your prospects in the shortest time. As with all of your other show activities, your mailing program should be carefully planned, with realistic goals and firm deadlines.

Your first mailing could be a simple letter thanking the prospect for visiting your booth and confirming the benefits of your product that were explained at that time. For a speedier reply you could send the letter by facsimile. Close the letter by promising a more personal contact in the near future or send a reply-paid card for use if fast action is required.

By sending such a letter, you have not only let prospects know that you value their interest in your product but you have also gained a little more time in which to follow up with a personal call or a telemarketing call to arrange a definite appointment. At this time, you should fulfill any promises that you made to the client.

Next, you should create a series of mailings at intervals, set to suit your business. The contents of the mailings would vary from letters and press releases, to specification sheets, catalogues, and flyers offering special deals. A great deal of creativity goes into the designing of mailing pieces. They should be designed to grab the reader's attention as discussed in chapter 6. Keep a file of flyers you receive in the mail — they will be a constant source of new ideas for your own efforts.

b. TELEMARKETING

The object of telemarketing is to make personal contact with the prospect. It also allows you to get in touch with a large number of prospects in the space of a few days.

Here are some guidelines to good telemarketing.

(a) Use people who understand what they are selling, speak clearly, and have a pleasant telephone manner

(b) Always identify the company. This serves two purposes: it tells the prospects who is calling — they are more likely to answer calls from companies they know than those they don't know; second, it serves as a constant reminder of your company name.

(c) If the telemarketer cannot answer a prospect's question, it should be noted and an answer provided within 24 hours if at all possible.

(d) Any promises made to a prospect should be logged, followed through, and reviewed by supervisors regularly.

(e) Use a bring-forward file to ensure that call-backs are made on the dates requested.

During the first contact, the telemarketer should thank the prospect for visiting your booth and quickly review your products and benefits. The telemarketer can then ask for an order, arrange an appointment for a salesperson to call, or arrange for the prospect to visit your show room. Later calls can introduce new products or new ideas, extend invitations to special events, or once again try to set up appointments.

c. PERSONAL SALES CALLS

Wherever possible, appointments should be made for personal calls. If you weren't able to fix a date at the show, then a phone call should be made either by the salesperson or by an experienced telemarketer. In the latter case, close cooperation between the salesperson and the telemarketer will be necessary to avoid conflicting appointments.

While setting up appointments is considered a common courtesy by many, you can't always get hold of people when you want to. If you are going to be in the area on a certain day, leave a message for the person saying you will try to contact him or her at that time. This approach has more chance of success than a straight cold call which many people regard as an unwarranted intrusion into their daily schedule.

By using a mix of each of these three methods, as determined by your particular situation, you can reap the full benefit of your efforts at the show and set the scene for an even more successful show next time.

14

POST-SHOW EVALUATION

Was it worth it? Should we do it again? What changes should we make? These are just three of the many questions you must answer once the show is over.

If you are to extract the full benefit from the show and maximize your investment, there are a number of things you should do in the days and weeks immediately following the show.

In chronological order, these things are —

(a) post-show debriefing,

(b) analysis of immediate results and comparison with goals,

(c) final analysis of costs and results and comparison with goals, and

(d) final report on show with recommendations for future shows.

These activities can be divided into two broad groups, subjective and statistical evaluations, each of which plays an important part in your overall assessment of the show.

Subjective evaluations tell you why and how things happened. They can come from a wide variety of people including your own staff, show staff, customers, competitors, and show visitors.

Statistical evaluations give you hard numbers against which you can compare your goals. They will come from your own staff and also from show management.

a. POST-SHOW DEBRIEFING

For maximum value, this should take place as soon as the show is over. Some companies prepare special evaluation forms for their booth staff to fill out immediately. This is particularly useful when staff have been drawn from different geographical locations and there is little probability of getting them all together again until the next show.

Other companies handle the debriefing by having a staff meeting, at which time evaluation forms may be filled out followed by a general discussion and recommendations for future shows.

Final analysis of costs and results

Whatever method is chosen, the review should take place while memories are still fresh in people's minds. A record of the comments and recommendations should be made for future use.

In addition to your own staff, valuable feedback can also be obtained from your customers and other visitors. You can do this by talking to them on the phone, sending them a questionnaire, inviting a representative group to a breakfast or luncheon meeting to discuss the show, or by employing an independent research company to do a survey for you.

Other sources of useful feedback are show managers, show services, competitors, and other exhibitors.

If you decide to prepare a questionnaire for your booth staff or others, it should be carefully thought out and structured. Here's a list of subjects that you might want to include in your questionnaire.

(a) Pre-show activities

Planning

Promotion

Training

Discussion of goals

Travel arrangements

Move-in

(b) At the show

Staffing and scheduling, technical back-up

Quality of booth

Comparison with competition

Caliber of demonstrations and displays

Staff knowledge, ability to answer questions

Staff behavior

Achievement of corporate goals

Literature and other materials

Signs and graphics

Lighting, floor coverings, location

Accessibility, show services, concessions

Traffic, audience quality

Registration and follow-up system

Any surprises?

Non-customer activities (students, agents, etc.)

Tear-down and move-out

(c) Post-show

Return and storage of booth

Lead follow-up

Accuracy and reliability of statistical data

Plans for next show

Overall impressions and recommendations

Since you are asking people for their thoughts and feelings, don't forget to express your appreciation for the time and effort that people spend.

b. ANALYSIS OF IMMEDIATE RESULTS

You should review the results immediately after the show and compare them with the goals that were set.

If your primary goal was to make sales at the show, count the sales. Your immediate follow-up action will be to make sure that all orders are dispatched without delay. If this is not possible, then customers should be notified of the delivery date and the order confirmed.

Where lead collecting was the primary goal, you should have a stack of lead cards or print-outs from the registration system. Whether you convert these leads into firm orders depends very much on your follow-up procedures (see chapter 13). However, your purpose at this moment is to compare the results statistically with your goals set before the show.

In preparing your statistics, you may find it helpful to sort the leads into several categories that match your goals. These might be —

(a) literature or catalogue requests,

(b) technical back-up,

(c) immediate buyer,

(d) medium-term buyer, and

(e) long-term buyer.

Compare the number of leads with the goals you set in different categories.

c. FINAL ANALYSIS OF COSTS AND RESULTS

Some weeks or months after the show, depending on your sales cycle, you should be able to bring together all of your costs and the full results from the show. These should be tabulated against your goals and budget for each item.

In addition to comparing the results with your goals, you should also be able to come up with statistics that will indicate how successful the show was for your company. By comparing your results with non-show sales costs, you will have a good yardstick by which to measure your current performance and predict that at future shows. Here are some examples of the kind of statistics you should be looking for:

(a) Number of sales calls required to close a show lead

(b) Cost of obtaining each lead (or sale) at the show

(c) Cost of each sale made as a result of the show

You can compare these results with your non-show costs of everyday business activities such as:

(a) Number of regular sales calls required to make a sale

(b) Cost of obtaining a sales lead through advertising or other forms of promotion such as direct mail

(c) Cost of each sale made as a result of non-show sales activities

When computing any of the above costs, (show or non-show), all relevant costs should be included, otherwise the results will be skewed and of little value. In particular, staff salaries and travel costs should be charged to the show budget and not buried in some other part of the marketing budget, as so often happens. The same applies to promotion and advertising.

Surveys have shown that the cost of obtaining a qualified lead at a show is about one-third of the cost of an industrial sales call. While these figures are averages, they do stress the importance of developing your own bench marks.

d. FINAL REPORT

Now is the time to bring together all of your information. This information should be summarized in one final report that will act as a guideline for planning future shows, setting goals, and determining which shows are effective and which shows you should pass up.

This final report should assess the following:

(a) The overall reaction of customers, staff, and others to your exhibit, highlighting strengths and weaknesses. Recommendations for extra training, new approaches etc., should be included.

(b) Comparison of actual costs to budget. This will highlight areas of weakness in budget controls and give firmer figures on which to base the next budget.

(c) Comparison of actual results to corporate and individual goals. This will point out areas of weak performance and the need for additional planning. Any shortfalls should be honestly assessed in terms of your own performance. Don't take the easy way out and blame the show management — unless the shortfall is common to most exhibitors.

Use Worksheet #5 to assess your performance at the show. Never lose sight of the fact that a show — trade or consumer — is a business proposition from start to finish. Plan it, execute it, and review it as you would any other business activity. If your show is successful, then you'll know how to go on to greater success next time. If the show fails to meet your expectations, you'll know why, and, more important, you'll know whether or not to participate in that show again, or alternatively what you need to do to be successful in future.

WORKSHEET #5
FINAL REPORT

Show_____

Dates_____Location_____

Comments from:	Strengths	Weaknesses
Customers_____	_____	
Staff_____	_____	
Others _____	_____	
Recommendations _____	_____	
_____	_____	

Costs (see Worksheet #2)	Actual $	Budget $	Difference (+) or(-)
Space rental	_____	_____	_____
Design & construction	_____	_____	_____
Transportation	_____	_____	_____
Show services	_____	_____	_____
Personnel	_____	_____	_____
Advertising & promotion	_____	_____	_____
Miscellaneous	_____	_____	_____

Goals
(see Worksheet #1)

	Results	Comments
1.	_____	_____
2.	_____	_____
3.	_____	_____
4	_____	_____
5.	_____	_____

15

CONCLUSION

The results of your show depend very much on you. You can achieve your corporate goals and chalk up a resounding success, or you can have a disappointing, unproductive marketing expense. Or it can be something in between these extremes.

Over 2,400 years ago, Sun Tzu wrote in *The Art of War* (edited by James Clavell, Delacorte, 1983) that the first rule of war is to plan your attack. "The general who wins a battle makes many calculations in his temple before the fight. The general who loses a battle makes but few calculations beforehand."

The same advice is applicable to exhibiting at trade and consumer shows.

Throughout this book, I have emphasized the importance of planning each stage of your show participation. Those who plan well in advance and have a firm understanding of what they are going to do and how they are going to do it will succeed.

Salespeople who appreciate the opportunities that shows offer approach shows with excitement and enthusiasm. Their attitude at the booth will make a big difference to your results. Properly trained booth staff will perform at their peak. These are the little things that give you a competitive edge.

Tzu comments on attitude that, "Whoever is first in the field and waits the coming of the enemy will be fresh for the fight; whoever is second in the field and has to hasten to battle will arrive exhausted."

Whether you meet your opponent on the battleground or the show floor, your needs are similar. To succeed, you must be ready.

Don't just read this book and file it away. Make it required reading for every member of your exhibition staff. Review it before each show.

Remember, a *Ready Buyer* is best met by a *Ready Salesperson*.

Good luck and excellent planning in all your future shows!

OTHER TITLES IN THE
SELF-COUNSEL BUSINESS SERIES

PROFESSIONAL SELLING: A WOMAN'S GUIDE
Surviving and thriving
by Carol Vipperman, B.A.

Women are becoming top producers in professional sales. Though it's still a predominantly male field, many companies now actively seek saleswomen because they possess inherently effective selling skills. This book helps women get ahead in this competitive, yet highly lucrative field. It shows women how they can turn their empathy, intuition, and superior communication skills into rewarding careers. The book is especially valuable for women who want to enter non-traditional fields. It also sheds light on problems that are frequently encountered and explains how to turn them into successes. A direct, concise resource book for the modern business woman.

Carol Vipperman writes from experience. As well as being a prolific writer, she is a successful consultant to business on selling and marketing strategies. She firmly believes that women can prosper in the business world of the nineties by integrating personal style with professional selling techniques. $9.95

KEEPING CUSTOMERS HAPPY
Strategies for success
by Jacqueline Dunckel and Brian Taylor

You need good service to attract customers and keep them coming back, and this book provides plans and programs that have been proven successful by other businesses. No matter what kind of business you are in, this book will help increase profits through improved customer relations. $8.95

Contents include:

- Customer service — what it is and what it is not
- The "why" of customer relations
- The value of service
- Developing a profitable customer relations program
- Setting goals for your business
- Putting your plan together
- Communicating your customer relations program to your employees
- Training employees
- Bringing it all together

BUSINESS ETIQUETTE TODAY
A guide to corporate success
by Jacqueline Dunckel

Mind your manners and get ahead! Knowing when to open the door for a colleague or how to accept a gift can sometimes mean the difference between being pigeon-holed in your current position or being offered that attractive promotion. But times have also changed, and the rules once relied on are not always appropriate today. With the growing number of women in company boardrooms and the move toward more international business, a new style of behavior is often called for.

This book is as easy to pick up and use as a quick reference before that special event as it is to read cover to cover. $7.95

Contents include:

- To begin at the beginning — the etiquette of employment

- Department decorum

- Telephone manners

- Meeting manners and boardroom behavior

- Introductions and conversation

- Cultural courtesy

- Table manners

- Eating in and dining out

- Giving and receiving — the etiquette of business gifts

- Put it in writing

ORDERING INFORMATION

All prices are subject to change without notice. Books are available in book, department, and stationery stores. If you cannot buy the book through a store, please use this order form. (Please print)

IN CANADA
Please send your order to the nearest location:
Self-Counsel Press, 1481 Charlotte Road,
North Vancouver, B. C. V7J 1H1

Self-Counsel Press, 2399 Cawthra Road, Unit 25
Mississauga, Ontario L5A 2W9

IN THE U.S.A.
Please send your order to:
Self-Counsel Press Inc., 1704 N. State Street
Bellingham, WA 98225

Name _____

Address _____

_____

Charge to:
❏Visa   ❏ MasterCard

Account Number _____

Validation Date_____

Expiry Date _____

Signature _____

❏**Check here for a free catalogue.**

Please add $2.50 for postage & handling.
WA residents please add 7.8% sales tax

In Canada, as of January 1, 1991, please add 7% GST to your order.

YES, please send me

_____copies of **Professional Selling: A Woman's Guide, $9.95**

_____copies of **Keeping Customers Happy**, $8.95

_____copies of **Business Etiquette Today**, $7.95